The Techniques of Decorating

The Techniques
of Decorating

Kevin McCloud

PHOTOGRAPHY BY
Michael Crockett

DORLING KINDERSLEY
LONDON • NEW YORK • STUTTGART

For Grace

Editors
Rosie Pearson
Mark Ronan
Sarah Lillicrapp

Designers
Steven Wooster
Sarah Ponder

First published in Great Britain in 1995 by Dorling Kindersley
Limited, 9 Henrietta Street, London WC2E 8PS

Copyright © 1995 Dorling Kindersley Limited, London
Text copyright © 1995 Kevin McCloud

Adapted from *Kevin McCloud's Decorating Book*
Copyright © 1990 Dorling Kindersley Limited, London
Text copyright © 1990 Kevin McCloud

A CIP record for this book is available from the
British Library

ISBN 0–7513–0180–9

Typeset by Tradespools, Somerset, UK.
Colour reproduction by Bright Arts, Hong Kong
Printed and bound in Singapore by C S Graphics

CONTENTS

INTRODUCTION • 8

PRINCIPLES
OF DECORATION

Getting ideas 14
Historical colours 16
Dividing wall space 18
Structural features 20
Using rhythm 22
Lighting, colour & mood 24
Whole house treatments 26

DECORATING
TECHNIQUES

Introduction • 28

SURFACES
Plaster & stone 30
Decorating plaster 32
Natural wood 34
Decorating wood 36
Paper & card 38
Metal & special finishes 40
Glass & plastic 42

TECHNIQUES
Simple decorative effects • 44
Colourwashing 46
Three-colour colourwashing 48
Colourwashing wood 50
Scrubbed limewash 52
Softened glazework 54
Patterned glazework 56
Liming wood 58
Spattering 60

Ageing & antiquing • 62
Ageing paint on wood 64
Craquelure 66
Antiquing 68
Antiquing plasterwork 70
Ageing plaster walls 72

Faux effects • 74
Pietra serena 76
Sandstone 78
Leather 80
Terracotta, plaster & lead 82
Verdigris 84
Iron & rust 86
Carrara & serpentine marble 88

Siena marble 90
Fossilstone marble 92
Clair bois 94
Graining with a brush 96
Graining with a rocker 98
Gilding – metal leaf 100
Gilding – metallic powder 102
Patinated gold 104
Stained glass 106

Painted pattern • 108
Making stencils 110
Using stencils 112
Stencil effects 114
Using photocopies 116
Grisaille 118
Trompe l'oeil 120

TOOLS, MATERIALS & DECORATOR'S REFERENCE

TOOLS
Decorating brushes 122
Fitches & lining brushes 124
Brushes for softening & varnishing 126
Specialist brushes, rockers & rollers 128
Stencils 130
Scrapers, spoons & other tools 132
Care of brushes 134

MATERIALS
Pigments & home-made paints 136
Proprietary paints 138
Varnishes & glazes 140
Solvents 142
Pastes & powders 144
Gilding materials 146

DECORATOR'S REFERENCE
Pigments & colours 148
Paints, varnishes & solvents 152
Recipes 156
Hints & tips 158
A list of terms & names 160
Guides to suppliers 164

Index • 170
Acknowledgments • 176

FOCUSING YOUR EFFORTS

The art of using enriched decoration has been too long forgotten and in its place rooms have been crammed with a confusion of all-over pattern. By concentrating your decorative energies on just one area of wall (in this case I chose a stick-on frieze) you can combine texture and colour to create a stunning focal point and transform the most ordinary room into something special.

INTRODUCTION

Decoration can be described as a superficial activity – literally surface deep, often intended to last only a few years and not essential to our existence. But it can give a great deal of pleasure, so why not learn to appreciate good decoration just as you appreciate good food? Contemporary taste in decoration comprises a new awareness of good design, a renewed confidence in handling rich and complex-looking decoration, and a greater interest in a wide variety of different diversification by manufacturers who, in the field of textiles alone, are producing everything from medieval reproduction damasks and eighteenth-century brocades to Victorian Arts and Crafts designs and ethnic weaves. And the same is true for furniture, accessories and fittings.

*T*ransforming a room with materials like paint and simple components like wood mouldings is, on the whole, inexpensive and quick, because it is only surface deep.*

Buy ornamental details as a short cut to
enriched decoration.

And though the techniques in this book will require a little more time than basic decorating, the sophisticated effects you create will more than repay your efforts. Another joy of working with paint and "stick-on" components is that nothing is irreversible: you can always "unpick" and readjust parts of a scheme, or a few years on start from scratch. The history of decoration is full of imitation and derivation. For centuries, decorators have cheated the eye, simulating expensive materials, like marble, with paint and imitating hand-painted details with paper cutouts. Decoration that relies heavily on special effects and unexpected materials to convey a strong sense of period or place is pure pastiche – this is something to celebrate because decorating should be fun!

REAPING THE BENEFIT

Just a few simple steps, and the most basic of materials will create an atmospheric and original scheme of decoration, the rewards of which far outstrip the little extra time spent.

EFFECTIVE ACCESSORIES

You only need one or two carefully chosen objects to root your decoration firmly in the period or place it echoes. These "hallmark" features, which should be given prominent positions, can take the form of three-dimensional ornaments or even photocopies.

Why not use marbled wrapping paper to make a frieze?

*M*y *views on decoration are close to those of William Morris, the Victorian designer and writer, who wrote that good decoration "has the impress of imagination strong on it" and is "something which can be done by a great many people and without too much difficulty and with pleasure". In decorating you have free rein to exercise your whims and fancies. The enjoyment you get every time you walk into a room might come from the satisfaction of knowing that it quietly conveys the atmosphere of a favourite historical period, or that it is flamboyant and theatrical (and why not, say, in a dining room or sitting room where guests are entertained?) This sort of decorating does, in terms of taste, expose your soft underbelly, but it does not matter in the least since decorating is not a public art like architecture; rather it is a private affair, so decorate for your own pleasure, not the approval of the outside world. I intend that this book should show you how to tread your own path confidently, with an armoury of decorating principles, techniques, and special tips at your disposal.*

Patterns and devices are often common to different periods.

GETTING IDEAS

SINCE EVERY room is different, each has its own starting point for decorating ideas. The quality of light varies from room to room, for reasons like the ceiling height and the number of windows. Some rooms may contain furnishings that you cannot fit anywhere else.

All these limiting factors are in fact departure points for creating a scheme. Throughout the techniques section, you will see rooms that are cluttered, sparsely furnished and that appear small and large. Each one makes a strong visual statement, which can sometimes mask a problem, or sometimes make a virtue out of necessity.

Transforming a room

I created a new decorative scheme for the sitting room in a late nineteenth-century house, shown in the snapshot below. In the bottom right-hand corner of the facing page you can see how the style of this room was reinterpreted in the flavour of the Arts and Crafts movement of the time, taking into account some of the inspirational materials on these pages.

Collecting reference

Inspiration for a decorating scheme can come from many sources: magazines, books, paintings, or even a piece of pottery. Hunt through old books, collecting images that take your fancy, and colour schemes that you admire, always bearing in mind the size of your room and the period of your house. You could also collect objects you particularly like, either for their colour or their shape, as well as paint-colour swatches and samples of papers, fabrics and flooring. As you build your little collection, so the identity of the room should become clearer.

Starting afresh

To help resolve the problem of how to decorate a room, it is useful to take a snapshot of the room and keep it for reference as you collect cuttings and other items of inspiration. Having a colour photograph in front of you helps to make problems seem a little more abstract; and by using felt-tip pens, you can draw suggested changes to the room directly on to the photograph before you actually begin decorating.

Magazine cuttings

Snapshot of room before decoration

Paint-colour swatches

Fabric with period design and colours

Inspirational objects, flooring and wall coverings

Stone for hearth

Stencil idea
for fireplace

Sample
wallpaper

Paint finish
for panelling

Colour
swatches
to match
wallpaper

Sample board of
limed floor

Final ideas

*As you gather inspiration, you should
begin to think about the relationships
that are going to spring up in the room
when you put your component elements
together. Think about how the colours
will work together. Consider using
natural surfaces such as plaster and
wood together, or combining slick
finishes such as polished wood and
marble. You may want to have a "user-
friendly" finish to your painted surfaces,
so think about ageing or antiquing them
slightly. When putting surfaces together,
it is always a good idea to make sample
boards of the finishes you intend to use
before starting.*

*For the decoration below I combined
a nineteenth-century Arts and Crafts
wallpaper with high panelling of
colourwashed wood. The result is a
modest room in light-reflective colours,
in which the natural qualities of wood
are exploited to establish a relaxed,
homely feeling.*

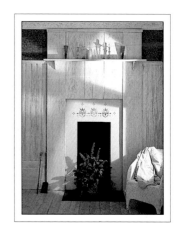

HISTORICAL COLOURS

WHEN YOU ARE choosing a scheme to decorate, you may want to use period colours. Several companies produce special ranges of paints in "historical" colours but these are not always accurate. The manufacturers usually rely on analyses of paint scrapings, which can be misleading because over time pigments can change colour. And, until this century, painters had no standard formulations for making up colours, and shades of a colour often varied depending on the local materials used. So trying to match the *exact* subtle shade of what you think is an authentic colour might well be a fruitless task! Instead, it is better to think of approximations and, as I often do in choosing paints, of colours that simply suggest a period. Here is some source material for historical colours (cuttings, reproduction fabric and wallpaper) along with standard modern paint swatches in similar colours.

Pale neo-Classical colours
As neo-Classicism became the rage in mid-eighteenth-century England, so the preferred colours of its innovator, Robert Adam, became popular. Usually placed against white, his muted tones of colours varied from intense and muddied greens and reddish purples, through to pastel combinations of exquisite subtlety. Look at architectural reference books for more of his ideas on colour combinations.

Eighteenth-century English neo-Classical colours

Frieze painted in neo-Classical colours

Taste of the early 1800s
Early-nineteenth-century French and English watercolours show a taste for strong, bright and somewhat unsubtle colours. Napoleon introduced the colours of Egypt – acid yellow and rich earth colours – to France and they were soon adopted into Empire taste. Deep pinks and mauves, however, were carried over from the previous century and they were translated, along with emerald green, into the English Regency stripe colours.

Swatches of some early-nineteenth-century colours

French colours
In France during the mid-eighteenth century, a taste for intense chalky-looking colours, particularly blues, greens and pinks, developed. To get as close a match as possible to the colours in the magazine cutting, above right, I laid cut-up paint swatches on top of the picture.

Swatches of mid-eighteenth-century French colours

Colours from fabrics

Original period fabrics that have been well preserved out of the light, or reproductions of period designs, are often a reasonably accurate source for historical colour. The fabric shown, right, is a modern version of an early American stencilled fabric notable for its ochre brown and glorious cranberry red.

Colour swatches that match stencilled fabric

Magazine cutting of an eighteenth-century frescoed room

Nineteenth-century wallpaper

Colours from wallpapers

The early nineteenth-century Gothic design, above, is still being made according to the designer's specifications, giving an accurate indication of the colour preferences of the period.

Looking at pigments

The colours of the artist's basic palette, unchanged for hundreds of years, were often those used by decorators. So I continue to use ancient palette colours in the form of powder colours and proprietary paints like emulsion.

Colour swatches to match wallpaper

Ultramarine blue similar to artists' oil paint colour

Swatch of modern paint colours

Ultramarine powder colour

Colours from magazines

Matching colours to magazine cuttings is an inexact science, but with care you can succeed in conveying the spirit of the age. The colours for the Rococo room on page 120, top left, were copied from a cutting of a frescoed room, above, dating from the right period, and are shown on the painted sample board beneath the magazine cutting.

Sample board for Rococo decor

Ultramarine artists' oil paint (an ancient palette colour)

DIVIDING WALL SPACE

ONCE SOME of the ideas for decorating your room have come together – maybe a period atmosphere you want to convey, the level of formality you require, or a completed colour scheme – start thinking about how you are going to articulate the wall space that you have before you.

A wall is like an empty canvas, which can be treated in any number of ways for different effects. Even though walls are flat, and the most usual treatment of them is two-dimensional, the overall effect of the wall decoration is much more powerful than that of floors or ceilings. This is because walls wrap around a room, enclosing the space between them. By manipulating the wall space, using division, colour and line as your tools, you can alter the character of a room.

Historically, walls have been subject to a number of horizontal divisions such as cornices and dado rails. These can be used separately or together, in similar or complementary colours to the wall, for different effects. The dado (the area between a skirting board and dado rail) is the place to make grand statements by using colours, textures and patterns that are different to the upper wall.

Floors and ceilings

When planning how to decorate the walls, think also about the floor and ceiling. The floor colour can work in tandem with the wall colour, either complementing or strengthening its effect, or it can be an entirely different colour, and act independently in the scheme.

Ceilings can also "float" independently from other structures in a room, although the colour of a ceiling can affect both the room's apparent height and lightness.

DADO EFFECTS

HORIZONTAL MOVEMENT

In this slice of wall taken from the Baroque scheme on page 50, top left, the dark panelled dado is slung very low above a pale floor. The resulting effect is of a slender green band, which serves to lead the eye horizontally around a room. This sets up a feeling of movement, which is then given a rhythm by the tassels and ropes at cornice height.

FORMAL DIVISIONS

Ebonized mouldings sharply delineate the divisions on the wall: the maroon frieze, the upper wall and wallpapered dado. The principal players here are the frieze and high skirting board that counterbalance each other at the top and bottom of the wall. This vertical relationship of all the parts is more important than any horizontal movement, and so the resulting atmosphere of the scheme is very formal and upright.

CRADLE OF COLOUR

In this nineteenth-century setting, the high dado of wooden panelling and the parquet-effect wood floor combine to make a cradle of colour that occupies the lower half of the setting and makes for a supportive, secure and friendly environment. The feeling of calm and stillness that this structure conveys can also be seen in settings of completely different periods.

BALANCE OF COLOURS

Here I used a high dado of pale plaster, topped with a rust-effect rail, to "fight off" a heavy blue wall. If the dado were any lower, it would have appeared crushed by the weight of the blue. As it is, it forms something resembling a wall, beyond which is the night sky. This is an example of how you can use the height of your dado to control the balance of colours in a room.

EFFECTS OF CEILING COLOUR

Brightening effect *By carrying the bright yellow of the dado up on to the ceiling, the effect is to open out the space and apparently raise the height of the ceiling. As a rule, light-reflective colours, like this yellow, are safest.*

Darkening effect *This blue ceiling echoes the colour of the wall, so pushing down on the yellow dado and seeming to lower the height of the setting. Dark ceiling colours should only be considered for strongly coloured rooms.*

Horizontal movement   Formal divisions   Cradle of colour   Balance of colours

STRUCTURAL FEATURES

PERIOD MOULDINGS help to structure a wall and enrich the decoration of a room. If you have a home in which cornices, friezes, dado rails or skirting boards have been partly ripped out during modernization, then a local timber mill will often match your existing mouldings and make up an exact quantity of "specials" for you.

Starting afresh

If your home has no authentic features left to restore (or they are beyond repair), simply use mouldings that are commercially available, where necessary combining them to imitate more complicated period mouldings. Not only is this cheaper than having specials run up, it can also be just as effective.

All the rooms in the techniques section were put together using materials and mouldings that were currently available from timber and plaster suppliers.

Historically, there has been a finite number of moulding patterns used in Western interior decoration. These have changed only in their scale and combination from one period to the next.

Modern manufacturers produce most standard period mouldings in many different sizes, which allows you to choose elements to suit your room. Some mouldings, with cross-sections, are shown here.

Shaker style

The American Shakers took great care over every single detail of their lives. Their rooms were not decorated for show and any detailing was there for practical reasons only. In the Shaker interior below I reproduced the mouldings found inside Shaker houses by carefully combining some commercially available mouldings. The pegboard is made from a simple plank, as is the deep dado rail (to prevent the backs of chairs scraping against the wall) but with the addition of an ogee panel moulding. I made the skirting from a plank with a rounded front edge and added beading along the top to prevent dust from settling, and pinned a small quadrant section at floor level to stop chair legs hitting the board.

Tudor decoration

In this Tudor setting, the principal wall decoration was composed of paint-textured hardboard panels and a painted frieze. But the walls needed a stronger structure to control these elements. I used a timeless dentilled cornice, a simple panel moulding to make dado-level rectangles and a modestly profiled board for the skirting.

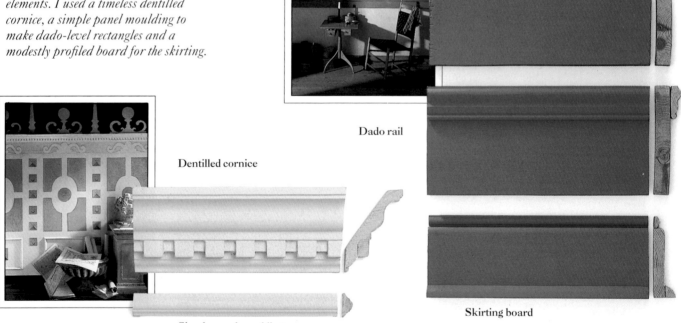

Pegboard

Dado rail

Dentilled cornice

Skirting board

Simple panel moulding

Profiled skirting board

Neo-Classical interior

The architecture of Robert Adam shows
a rare sensitivity for the combined use of
mouldings, enriched decoration and
colour. His interiors were decorated in a
variety of different materials, such as
composition or fibrous plaster, painted
wood, and papier-mâché. *Similarly,*
the interior I put together makes use of
mouldings produced in different media.
The frieze is lincrusta, a nineteenth-
century invention, finished with a plastic
picture rail beneath. There is a plaster
dado rail, then a skirting board made
from a plank of wood topped with a
machine-made moulding.

Dentilled cornice

Dado rail

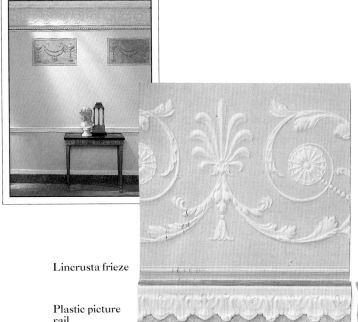

Lincrusta frieze

Plastic picture
rail

Plaster dado rail

Machine-made
moulding

Base for
skirting board

Tongue-and-groove
matchboarding

Skirting board

Caribbean setting

In this Caribbean setting I captured a
little of the atmosphere of the region, and
the result was a mixture of ethnic func-
tionalism with a little touch of the
Colonial. The same dentilled moulding
as I used in the Tudor setting proved an
accurate copy of a Jamaican Colonial
cornice, and works surprisingly well in
combination with the simple painted
matchboarding (topped with a dado
rail) beneath it. Continuing the use of
basic materials, you will notice how the
skirting board is just a simple plank of
wood, painted with emulsion.

USING RHYTHM

THE MOST underrated technical effect available when decorating, is visual rhythm, which can bounce some life into a room. Its use provides a rich vein to be tapped, and one that has been neglected too long, since enriched decoration fell from grace in the early part of the twentieth century.

At its simplest, rhythmic decoration can be two symmetrically placed windows in a room, which you decide to dress up and show off, or it might be two matching mirrors placed in a prominent and symmetrical position. This has a visually satisfying effect because it defines and emphasizes the space between and on either side of the two features.

Repeated images

At its most complicated and diffused, rhythm can be seen in wallpapers and fabrics, sending off little repeats in all directions.

Images or motifs, repeated so that they pulse around a room, set up an obvious rhythm and act as a meter by which all the components of the room can be judged. The strength of its impact depends on the scale of the images you use and the number of repeats in relation to the size of the room.

Horizontal rhythms

Sometimes, as in the examples opposite, the most obvious and exciting rhythms are those that run in just one direction, horizontally around the room. Their energies are not dissipated and they follow the architecture of the room. They are also all placed at cornice height so the repeated motifs can be clearly seen and do not become confused with any other decoration in the room. It is important that furniture, wallhangings and people do not get in the way of the flow of the pattern, or the rhythm will cease.

SUBTLE MOVEMENT

This Classical lincrusta frieze has a complex design that is repeated every half a metre. Because it is low relief and painted in restrained colours, the potential rhythmic impact is reduced.

SWINGING RHYTHM

A repeat of tassels and rope can be left unfettered by background or frame. The images are large and simple and the repeat is bold and swinging. This waveform repeat will add life to a room.

RHYTHMIC IMAGERY

To pick up on the imagery of a balloon chandelier, I pasted equally-spaced colour photocopies high on to the wall. The chandelier helps identify what the image is: a sedate rhythm made up of separate beats, to give focus to the central balloon.

MULTIPLE PATTERNING

This pattern is so complicated that any energy in the repeat is dissipated. The wave pattern of the rope is complicated by the frequency of its repeat, by the brightly painted moulding, and by the vertical stripes on the wall. Yet the combination, although lacking in rhythmic power, is rich and decorative.

BALANCED COMPOSITION

A principal repeat of the bird strikes an obvious rhythm here, linked and balanced by a chain of tiny details. The zig-zag above serves as an angular wave-form, setting up a more frequent repeat. Strong rhythms within rhythms set up the visual equivalent of the resonance of sound.

GENTLE WAVES

The wave shape is a simple rhythmic device, and can be in the form of a rope, a swag, a garland or, as here, a chain. These materials come in flexible lengths, so you can adjust the distance between the "waves" until you have the right repeat for the room.

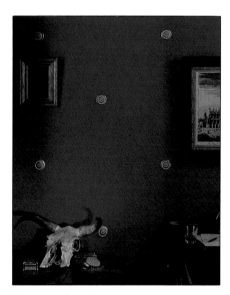

Repeated studs
These gilded studs were attached to the wall in the Victorian scheme on page 60. The idea of using relief decoration was to assert the repeats in a very strong fashion. The studs are widely spaced and give a healthy rhythmic feel to the decoration of the room.

Rhythmic panelling
In this example of all-over rhythmic wall decor, different rhythms run in varying directions all at once. However, the divisions in the main wall panelling do correspond to the simpler repeated rhythm shown above it, and work in a strictly geometrical pattern.

LIGHTING, COLOUR & MOOD

THE MOST common assumptions made about the colours of rooms are misleading. For example, the most light-reflective and cheerful colours are not just pale peach and apricot, as is popularly believed, but also bright yellow and lavender blue. If you try to modulate the atmosphere of a scheme simply by lightening its colour, you run the risk of introducing more light at the expense of the setting's character.

Before choosing a colour, consider whether you spend more time in a room by day or in the evenings. Most colour schemes look good under artificial lighting. If your problem is a dingy room by day, try adding mirrors and complementary colours (see p.160) before you consider using a pale colour scheme.

In the setting shown on these pages, the brown version (below) is most arcane and interesting. By day it is less light-reflective (bottom), but the colour responds well to daylight and makes the room seem warm and inviting. The pale scheme (right and far right), on the other hand, is less appealing by day, when it seems relatively cold and lifeless, but at night, by candlelight, it becomes magical.

Effects of colours
To demonstrate the effects of colours I repainted the same wood-panelled wall in two different colours. First of all I colourwashed it in white over blue stained wood (above and right). It was then stripped and colourwashed in a soft brown (below and left). In both instances it was possible to use the wood's texture to add interest to the painted surface, and by comparing the two photographs taken in daylight, you can immediately see that this surface interest has more influence than the colour of the paint on the setting's character. Although the brown-coloured wall darkens the room, it conveys more atmosphere than the colder blue.

WHOLE HOUSE TREATMENTS

DECORATING should be fun and enjoyable. It does not always involve major restructuring, nor should it, since in every sense of the word it is a superficial activity. All the room sets in this book are broad interpretations of styles from different countries and periods. They are not historical documents, and each one could look at home in half a dozen different types of house of different ages. If you decorate with a sense of fun, you will appreciate this.

Developing a theme

But how can you take an idea that you like for one room, and then decorate the whole house? What will give your home an identity that can assume different guises in different rooms?

The need for this variation is obvious, since we are different people when we are entertaining, to when we are in private rooms such as the bathroom or bedroom, to when we come home from work: and accordingly we make different demands on our environment. But equally, homes are single dwelling units, and far too many people decorate their homes as though the rooms were hermetically sealed and independent of each other.

On these pages are shown the three thematic principles to bear in mind when decorating a whole house, namely colour, materials and period. Using just one of them as a criterion will help you formulate a look for the inside of your house that should have some integrity. If you are able to use all three together, and make all the rooms conform by colour, materials and period, your home will grow in character even more.

Period homes

Decorating a period house can be fraught with crises of conscience. Is what you are doing right for the period of the building? Are you using the correct materials and colours? Or if what you are doing is not authentic, only interpretive, does it respect the fabric and character of the building?

How to decide

These questions are valid to some extent, particularly in valuable old houses. But decorating is a private activity and its aim is personal enjoyment; it has always reflected the tastes of individuals, not public bodies, and it should remain so. The most important consideration facing anyone decorating a period home is not what should or should not be added, but what should or should not be taken away.

The answer is to remove as little as possible of the original structure because whatever is added to a building in terms of mouldings and paint is reversible, but original features, once ripped out, cannot easily be replaced. The domestic vandalism of many nineteenth-century homes during the 1960s has meant that what is now being replaced and restored is often inaccurate and out of tune with what was probably there originally.

Choosing by colour

One of the simplest ways of carrying a theme through your whole house is by following a common colour scheme throughout. This does not mean that you should use exactly the same colour in every room, rather it is a question of choosing a colour palette and working around those colours. In the choice below, I combined colours from the orange/red end of the spectrum, which were used in Victorian, Oriental and Spanish-style settings. Each of the settings has different finishes and surface qualities. The Victorian wall is painted a deep red and spattered with paint and glaze (p.60, top left); and the wall from the Moorish bedroom has been given a dusty terracotta finish (p.82, top left).

Red background spattered with glaze and paint

Saffron-red softened glazework, above

Wall with terracotta paint finish, left

Choosing by materials

By adopting one principal material as your decorative linking component, you can experiment with using a wide range of colours. Here I chose textured plaster as a wall finish that you could use all over the house. The schemes illustrated here have a French/Hispanic theme. Although each was designed for a specific room in a house (a bedroom, a kitchen and a living room) they could be adapted to work equally well in other rooms.

Stencilled plaster for a French kitchen scheme

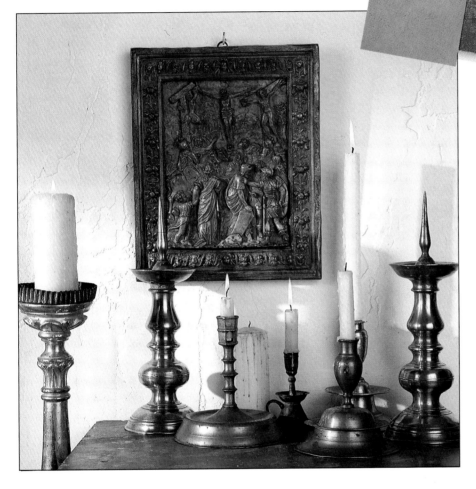

Whitewashed plaster wall in a seventeenth-century Spanish bedroom setting, left

Painted plaster in a twentieth-century scheme, below

Colour, material and period

The strongest link between rooms is formed when you contrive to link them in more than one way. The sequence here shows rooms linked by a colour palette of greens, a common material of painted wood, and a common root in their styles; the English setting is based on the simple seventeenth-century style of interior that influenced early American interiors.

New England interior

Seventeenth-century English setting

American Colonial setting

DECORATING TECHNIQUES

To master the techniques in this book, first practise them. Wall finishes can be tried out on the wall you are going to decorate and painted over in white. You can also practise techniques that use transparent oil glaze on the surface to be decorated as long as you wipe it off before it dries. Experiment with waxes and pastes on scrap wood. To get an impression of different colours, prepare large sample boards and hold them up in different parts of the room. The effect of any colour is intensified when all four walls are painted the same; to judge the impact of this, paint the inside of an old paint can (see opposite). I never apply paint with a roller because the texture spoils subsequent paint layers. Quantities for mixing materials are given as proportions (to dilute eggshell paint 1:4 with white spirit, for example, use four times the volume of white spirit as paint). Information on making paints, tinting emulsion and eggshell, estimating quantities and special tips on glazework and finishing are included on pages 156–59.

Home-made tool for painting straight edges

Colour sample boards

Airtight container useful for storing powders

Electric sander, and paint tin in a paint kettle

Setting up and finishing

Always lay down plenty of dust sheets and put paint tins in paint kettles to catch drips (this also makes it easier to carry tins without a handle). Attach the paint kettle to the ladder with a snap-hook. Always work in a well-ventilated area and do not drink, eat or smoke. Certain materials should only be used with rubber gloves, goggles or a mask (dust masks prevent powder particles from being inhaled; use a special respiratory mask to avoid inhaling fumes if using solvents). Safety tips are given with each technique and on pages 148–55. If you stop for an hour or so, cover your brushes with a rag dampened with water (for water-based paints) or with turpentine (for oil-based paints). Clean your brushes and close all paint containers before finishing for the day.

Thick rubber gloves

Long ruler and spirit level

Plastic paint kettle attached with a snap-hook

Colour test in empty paint container

On the workbench: dust mask and protective goggles

PLASTER & STONE

THE PRIMITIVE quality and archaeological associations of bare rough plaster, stone, marble and terracotta are most suited to rooms with a Mediterranean, country/ethnic, ancient or medieval slant. But polished marble and some glazed terracotta, particularly when they are laid in complex patterns, are also suited to rooms decorated in a grander, neo-Classical style.

Appreciating uneven plaster

Old, crumbly plaster walls make such an atmospheric alternative to flat, plainly painted walls that I devised a special technique (see pp.72–73), in which new plaster is applied and textured to resemble genuinely old walls. The plaster should be mixed in a bucket as shown below.

Flat plaster

Smooth plastering is a highly skilled operation and usually best undertaken by a professional plasterer. Small holes or unwanted cracks, however, can easily be disguised with filler (a fine plaster, available in small quantities).

Tools

To apply new plaster you need a trowel, for filling cracks, a scraper, and for scraping off loose plaster, a shavehook. Hemp scrim together with fibreglass make up the fibre in cast plasterwork, like the moulding at the top of the page.

Plaster moulding

Scraper

Hemp scrim

Shavehook

Trowel

WORKING WITH PLASTER

Mixing plaster *Shake plaster into water until it peaks just above the surface. Mix and then transfer to an upturned dustbin lid for working.*

Stabilizing *Old and flaking plaster walls, distemper and old porous paint should be brushed with stabilizing solution before decorating.*

Filling *To fill small cracks, rake out any loose plaster, dampen the surface and apply new plaster or filler with a scraper. Sand flat when dry.*

Plaster mouldings

Decorative plaster is an essential element of many period styles. Standard designs, like the one above, are readily available from most DIY stores and builder's merchants; less common designs can be obtained from specialist suppliers. In the last century, mouldings were made in position (a basic frame was shaped and precast enrichments plastered in), but today they are usually precast in quick-setting gypsum plaster. They should be plastered into walls (by a professional) or, in the case of lighter mouldings, screwed in.

Black granite

Terracotta tile

Serpentine marble, left

African slate floor tiles, above

Terracotta tiles

Made from fired clay, terracotta is perhaps the warmest coloured building material and suits country and Mediterranean style interiors, in particular. To appreciate its natural qualities, use it in the form of clear-glazed or unglazed wall or floor tiles (the latter should be bedded in sand and cement). Alternatively, reproduce the qualities of terracotta with paint (see pp.82–83) and varnish the finish to make it hardwearing. Or, colour concrete tiles with woodstain and coat them with matt varnish.

Marble and stone

Marble is the name given to any stone that can be polished to a hard, glossy finish, including granite. Scagliola (a dough of pigment, lime, marble dust and glue) is a traditional fake-marble material. Paint has long been used to imitate marble – the price of real marble makes this or the use of marble offcuts popular (some marbles scratch too easily to be used for floors). Other stones that can be used for floors include slate and sandstone.

DECORATING PLASTER

MANY DECORATIVE paint effects, such as colour-washing and patterned glazework, are suitable for smooth (and sometimes rough) plaster walls. The preparation required for special paint effects varies; details are given with each technique.

Decorative mouldings

Plaster also comes in the form of mouldings, which have formed an integral part of many interiors since the eighteenth century. As an alternative to painting these (and possibly glazing them too, as shown on pp.54–55), I devised a simple method of antiquing (pp.70–71), which gives plasterwork a natural-looking, mellow bloom.

Types of plaster

Most modern decorators' plasters are gypsum plasters. Quick-setting plaster of Paris (some mouldings are cast from these and it is useful for repairing them) is one form of gypsum plaster and there is a range of slower-drying varieties. Wall plasters are sold in two grades (bonding and finishing coat) or as a one-coat plaster, and come in many colours. Modern plaster powders absorb water and if used after a month or two of storage will dry faster, making work difficult.

Plaster for walls and mouldings can be mixed with powder colours. Follow the instructions on page 157 and only use alkali-resistant colours (these are listed on pp.148–51).

Traditional plaster is made of lime, sand and often horsehair or some other fibre. Old houses that have never had a damp-proof course should be plastered with a traditional lime-based plaster and then painted with distemper (see p.156) to allow for the natural evaporation of moisture.

Drying out

Freshly plastered walls or newly cast decorative plasterwork should be allowed to dry out for several weeks (or ideally several months) before decorating, to allow for the full evaporation of moisture from the surface; otherwise the paint may bubble and flake off.

Preparing bare plaster

Bare plaster that is to be painted with emulsion should be sealed with PVA or a coat of emulsion diluted to half its strength with water. Before painting with oil-based paints, coat the plaster with PVA or an alkali-resistant primer. Shellac is an alternative sealant that can be used before applying both water-based and oil-based paints.

Painting in plaster
Fresco is one of the oldest types of painting; a mixture of powder pigment and water is applied to a coat of half-set, freshly applied lime plaster. As the plaster dries it absorbs the wet paint, bonding it into the top layer. I painted the cherub fresco above in this way using alkali-resistant powder colours (these do not fade in contact with lime).

Gilded plaster *This cherub, cast in plaster of Paris, was sealed with a coat of shellac, sprayed with red oxide spray paint and gilded with metal leaf.*

IMITATION STUCCOWORK

I dipped rope in plaster of Paris to match the tassels and give the appearance of stuccowork.

Antiqued plaster cornice

Antique finish
One of the most effective ways of decorating fresh plaster-work is with shellac and liming wax (see the antiquing technique on pp.70–71). The resulting alabaster-like sheen belies the relative cheapness of the actual materials underneath. The technique is as suitable for large areas of plasterwork, such as the cornice above, as small plaster mouldings. It is important to leave small castings for several days before antiquing, to allow moisture to evaporate.

Casting plaster
Plaster mouldings can be bought in a variety of styles or you can experiment with casting your own. Use plaster of Paris and mould-making materials from craft shops. I made the tassel, below left, and coated the plaster with shellac. When this was dry, it was painted with red and brown French enamel varnishes (see p.141). To show up the highlights I rubbed off some of the dry French enamel varnish with a little methylated spirits. Alternatively, castings can be painted or antiqued like the cornice shown above.

Using other materials
Even wooden or plastic mouldings, like the shapes on the left (which I bought from a decorating supplier) can be paint-finished to look like old plaster. This makes it possible to make really fine ornament (which it is not possible to cast from plaster) fit in with other antiqued features in a room.

Plastic castings with a pink plaster paint finish

Home-made plaster casting

Corbels and bowl
The technique used on the cornice at the top of the page is just as effective on the corbels and bowl, right. These mouldings would be at or near ceiling height but the resulting finish is so soft and beautiful and can withstand such close scrutiny that it warrants use on eye-level objects too. So satisfying is the finish that it encourages you to buy castings to hang on your wall, like the panels on page 120, top left.

Antiqued corbels

Antiqued bowl

NATURAL WOOD

WOODS THAT have been treated so that the natural character of the grain can be appreciated (either by varnishing, polishing or oiling with a clear medium) have a friendly and warm appearance. Before applying standard varnishes (see pp.140–41), wood should first be prepared as described, right. Beeswax furniture polish nourishes wood as well as giving it a pleasing, soft finish and a scent of honey.

Choosing wood

The world is being depleted of more natural forest than can be replaced, so buy wood that comes from a renewable source, such as pine from Scandinavia, in preference to Brazilian hardwoods, which come from tropical rain forests.

If you plan to paint wood the standard way or to woodgrain it (the latter is shown on p.153) you will obliterate its natural qualities anyway, so consider using fibreboard, chipboard or hardboard, all of which are products of timber waste.

Most softwoods such as pine and spruce are relatively inexpensive and hence popular in the home. Some have an attractive grain, which you may choose to enhance by giving a clear finish, but often it is not particularly interesting and looks best when painted.

Hardwoods, such as oak, elm, ash, walnut, beech and mahogany are, as their name suggests, harder, and they have subtler and prettier grains. Because of their cost they are more common for furniture and mouldings than large areas, such as flooring and panelling, and they are often polished to beautiful natural finishes rather than painted.

Softwood mouldings

The architrave moulding below is an example of the extensive range of widely available low-relief stamped mouldings. They make an inexpensive alternative to machine-carved mouldings, or the even more superior hand-carved mouldings. Because their finish is often rather coarse they are usually best painted. Use screws or nails to attach them.

Oil-based varnish

Knotting

Preparing and varnishing wood

Use varnish to protect wood and allow the natural grain to show through. I prefer oil-based varnish to polyurethane varnish, which has a tendency to yellow. To prevent resin seeping from knots in the wood, apply knotting (which will darken the wood slightly) or white polish (which is less effective but will not darken the colour). A coat of shellac-based sanding sealer will prevent the varnish from colouring the wood.

Softwood architrave moulding

Narrow mouldings

These are widely available, either simply shaped or patterned. They can be used singly or in combination, as dado rails, to enrich standard skirtings or at picture rail height. Softwood examples look most effective stained, painted or glazed, while mouldings made from hardwoods, such as mahogany and oak, are best polished with wax or varnished so their grain can be fully appreciated.

Stamped softwood moulding

Softwood ogee moulding

Softwood panel moulding

Olive wood

Turned ash nutbowl

Hardwoods

Oak, elm and mahogany are amongst the most widely used hardwoods and are often used to make highly polished mouldings. They are expensive (and mahogany should be used sparingly because it is a tropical wood) but small amounts look effective in conjunction with softwoods stained or woodgrained to match (woodgraining techniques are shown on pp.94–99). Sycamore and fruit woods, such as cherry, are usually used for inlay, veneers and for turning.

Oak

Mahogany

Qualities of ash *This hardwood is a popular wood for decorative objects and furniture veneers because of its attractive grain pattern, which remains highly pronounced even when it is stained, colourwashed (see pp.50–51), limed (see pp.58–59), or even sprayed black. It is turned, to make objects like the nutbowl above; less expensive woods, like pine, are usually inadequate for turning because the high number of knots in the wood catch against the turning blade and sometimes shatter the wood.*

Darkened oak beam

Old oak

In the Middle Ages, oak beams were sometimes protected with pitch, or whitewashed (so if you paint oak beams white you will be following an ancient tradition). But most were left bare and darkened naturally with time (over the last 150 years there has been a vogue for artificially darkening old beams).

DECORATING WOOD

THERE ARE several techniques for colouring wood that, far from disguising its natural characteristics, serve to enhance them. But standard coats of paint can also be used to great effect, particularly on mouldings and panelling. In the room on page 50, the character of the wood is subjugated, so that the Classical composition of forms stands out.

First steps

Before painting, the knots in resinous woods should be brushed with knotting to prevent the seepage of resin. The knots in the pine that forms the background here, were treated with white polish (see p.141) rather than knotting (which is dark brown) so as not to spoil the

subtle pale-pink colourwashing. Except in the case of colourwashing and ageing paintwork, wood that is to be painted or limed should be sealed with sanding sealer, or primed, lightly sanded (in liming, the wood is wire-brushed instead) and then undercoated. Previously painted wood should be cleaned with sugarsoap first, and gloss paint lightly sanded. Varnished wood should be stripped.

Imitation wood

Cast resin is often less expensive than wood. Some companies make resin panelling that can be used to clad an entire room. Because the moulds are taken from wood originals the reproduction of grain and pattern is realistic.

Colour-washed wood

Colourwashing wood

This simple technique, using thin washes of diluted paint, gives wood a soft, almost milky-looking appearance. The advantages over using woodstain are that you have a far wider choice of colours and can control the amount of grain you see.

Cast resin "carving"

Wood-effect flooring

Some types of plastic flooring have a pattern and surface finish that is almost indistinguishable from real wood. This is a suitable alternative to painted and/or varnished wood for bathroom floors because it does not lift or stain.

Pickled (limed) pine floorboards

Aged paint finish on matchboarding

Plastic wood-effect flooring

Imitation woodgrain

For centuries, paint has been used to imitate different woodgrains, either on non-wood surfaces or on wood, which provides a natural underlying pattern. The paler grain effects, right, were executed on plywood; the dark example is beech with a paint-simulated rosewood grain. Woodgraining (see pp.94–99) can be used to make some woods like pine resemble more expensive hardwoods, and to unify non-wood surfaces with other elements in a room; see the woodgrained bath on page 94, top left, for example.

Dark oak-grain effect on plywood

Plywood painted to resemble light oak

Beech with a painted rosewood grain

The effect of liming on a carved oak panel

Liming wood

Liming is one of the simplest and most stunning ways to treat wood. The wax or paste with which the wood is rubbed, leaves a faint white deposit in the wood's pores, accentuating the natural grain pattern; it can look particularly effective on carved surfaces, where it sticks in the recesses. Woods that have an open grain, like ash, oak and elm, are the easiest to grain; woods like pine, which have a closed grain, need to have their grain artificially opened by vigorous and repeated wire-brushing. The technique is shown on pages 58–59.

Aged paint finish

Wood can be given a peeled and chipped paint finish. The yellow emulsion paint on the matchboarding, left, was applied over blobs of wax, which resisted the paint, allowing it to be rubbed off to reveal patches of wood (see pp.64–65).

PAPER & CARD

Photocopy of
a gryphon

FOR MANY centuries, paper decoration has been used in houses and is still very popular today. There are three main ways paper is used, the most obvious being surface decoration on walls and objects, for example wallpapers, borders and *découpage*. Another use is to screen and filter light, for instance when paper is stretched on a frame and treated with oils. Finally, paper can be used as a technical decorating aid, such as in stencilling and tracing.

being lining paper, which can be used either underneath decorated wallpaper or as a base for paint. In the eighteenth century, lining paper was often glued directly over wooden boarding and then painted in imitation of more expensive wallcoverings. The first printed wallpapers also imitated other surfaces, such as tapestry, wall paintings and stretched fabric.

For best results, always use conventional wallpaper pastes (or PVA for *découpage*) when pasting paper.

Wallpaper
The most familiar type of paper decoration is wallpaper. There are many forms, the simplest one

Photocopy decoration
Glue photocopies of unusual designs on to furniture or walls for a cheap form of découpage (see pp.116–17).

Classical paper border

Paper borders
These are traditionally printed on heavy-duty paper and often come in long rolls. You can easily make your own borders, however, by sticking together repeated photocopies. Placed either at frieze height or dado level, borders can add that extra touch of style.

Stencils
Some modern stencils are cut out from acetate sheet, which is tough as well as being flexible enough to go round corners. But it is slippery, so can be difficult to cut. Stencil card (also called oiled manila card), is the traditional material, and is tough and thick.

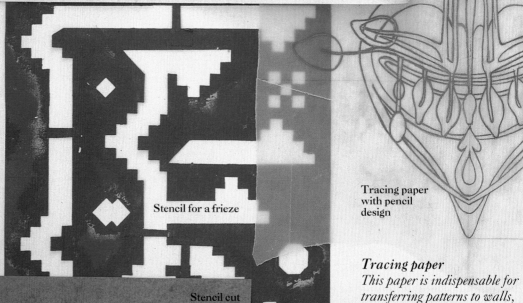

Stencil for a frieze

Stencil cut from oiled manila card

Tracing paper with pencil design

Tracing paper
This paper is indispensable for transferring patterns to walls, floors and furniture. Designs are first traced on to the paper and then the pencil outline of the image is transferred to the surface by rubbing the back of the tracing with pencil.

Wallpaper with
nineteenth-century
design

Tissue paper

Oiled tissue
paper

Floral
wrapping
paper

Colour découpage
*Inexpensive gift paper,
though very thin, can be
cut out, glued and then
applied to walls or pieces
of furniture. For repeated
images you can use colour
photocopies. Protect the
découpage with a coat of
clear varnish.*

Oiled tissue paper
*When paper is coated with
varnish, oil or shellac, it
becomes translucent. Use
oiled tissue paper to make
screens for windows; coat
lining paper with shellac
for lampshades (see p.156).*

Victorian style border

Brown
paper

Wallpaper
*Although it can be expensive, wallpaper
offers an immense range of patterns.
You can choose between pictorial papers,
like the Victorian frieze above, or flat,
graphic designs like the nineteenth-
century Gothic design, top.*

Brown paper
*This was sometimes used instead of
patterned wallpaper in late nineteenth-
century Arts and Crafts interiors, which
were simply decorated and furnished; see
pages 24–25.*

METAL & SPECIAL FINISHES

IN THE home, metal takes the form of radiators, pipes, and door and light fittings. It looks effective bare, painted or even corroded; the natural decorative patinas of rust, verdigris and gold can be imitated on metal and non-metal surfaces.

Protecting metal

Many metals (gold is one exception) tarnish on exposure to air. Iron and steel turn to rust, and copper and brass tarnish, or turn green to form verdigris. You can prevent rust on bare metalwork with a rust-inhibiting primer, which can then be undercoated and painted over with gloss or eggshell. To appreciate the natural qualities of metals,

simply protect with a layer of either varnish or metal lacquer.

To make the most of the highly decorative appearance of chemical change, place differently patinated metals together for stunning visual effects or imitate them on metal, plastic, wood or plaster. The techniques for imitating iron, rust and verdigris are on pages 84–89.

Gold

Because of the cost of solid gold, for centuries it has been beaten into wafer-thin layers, or leaves, and used to gild all sorts of surfaces. The art of gilding (see pp.100–101) is worth mastering, if only because of the sheer pleasure to be derived from handling metal leaf.

Priming metal

Metal must be primed and undercoated before being painted (if the metal has been lacquered, first strip it with a chemical stripper). For iron and steel use red oxide primer, shown on the radiator below; this is a specially formulated oil-based primer.

Rusty fire-tongs

Decorative rust
Why not view rust as a naturally-occurring decorative finish? These iron fire-tongs, once too brash and shiny for the room they occupied, were left outside for a month and then, to prevent the rust progressing, polished with beeswax polish (beeswax has anti-rusting properties).

Gilding
Use gold leaf to bring the shine and richness of gold to metallic and non-metallic surfaces. On carved pieces, like these plastic ornaments gold leaf really catches the light; the effect here was furthered by gilding over a coloured ground, which shows through the leaf.

Gilded plastic ornaments

Verdigris paint finish on a pipe joint

Red oxide primer

Copper and verdigris
Copper bathroom pipework looks extremely effective unpainted, lacquered with metal lacquer and polished to a shine. Corroded metal, in the form of real verdigris or a verdigris paint finish (like that on the pipe's joint above), looks good with polished metal.

Sprayed plastic anthemion

Effects on non-metals
Paint is the cleanest and safest way of emulating metal patinas (alternative processes involve using highly toxic chemicals). The plastic motif, left, was sprayed gold for quick effect and varnished. More complex patinas that can be imitated with paint include cast iron, shown on the piece of lincrusta, left, and rust shown on the strip of wood, left.

Rust effect on wood

Painted metal lamp

Patterned paint finish
There are several specialized metallic paints that give a patterned finish on metals and non-metals, like wood. One such is the hammer-finish enamel paint used on the lamp, above, which gives a beaten metal effect when brushed out. Most metallic paints are tough and quick-drying, but have toxic solvents.

Cast iron effect on lincrusta

Antiqued doorknob

Antiquing metals
New brass, and surfaces gilded with metal leaf, can sometimes look too brash. French enamel varnish can be applied to most metal surfaces for an antiquing effect. Dilute it 1:1 with methylated spirits and sponge it on, as I did on the brass doorknob above, or spatter it, as I did on the gilded urn on the opposite page. The method of antiquing metal leaf and metallic powder is shown on page 102.

Gold and metal finishes
The most unlikely surfaces can be given the appearance of metal. For the lincrusta dado above I used water-based washes and for the verdigris effect, gold powders, and French enamel varnish.

Lincrusta panel decorated with metallic powders and verdigris paint finish

GLASS & PLASTIC

GLASS IS a beautiful and varied medium, with many decorative uses in the home. It is available moulded and pressed, polished, coloured and painted, patterned, etched and sand-blasted. Yet whatever form it takes, glass retains its essential qualities of hardness, brittleness and translucency.

The relationship between glass and light is intrinsic to how glass performs; it is a modifier of light and so its role in the interior is an important one. The positioning of glass in a room should primarily be in response to the light source in that room, so that glass vases are backlit with light from windows, and mirrors repeat the imagery of the windows, in their shape, size, and reflections.

An undervalued material

It might be thought that plastic is a poor substitute material, and in fact the qualities of plastics that are imitative of glass are poor; they scratch, do not refract light into the spectrum colours and are prone to a build-up of static electricity that attracts dust. But there are hundreds of other plastics available, some of which possess unique characteristics; their use should not be dismissed lightly.

The argument against using plastics is that they are fake, cheap and mass-produced, and they are not sympathetic companions to the otherwise "natural" materials used in building. But plasticizers are used today in concrete, plaster and paint. And the pedigree of plastics is an old one: Robert Adam, the eighteenth-century English architect, asked several companies to manufacture component wall decorations in either *papier-mâché* or composition (a mixture of rosin, glue and whiting) that performed the role of more expensive carved wood. Two linseed oil-based products, linoleum and lincrusta, which can also be seen as prototype plastics, followed in the nineteenth century. All these materials have pleasant handling properties.

Stained glass effect
One way to control the quality of light in your room is to paint your own stained glass (see pp.106–107).

Cast resin decoration
The use of high-quality silicone rubber moulds ensures faithful reproduction of every detail of the wood-like platerack, right. There should be few qualms about using cast resin decoration, such as this, because even the use of moulds to cast plaster decoration can be seen as a way of imitating carving.

Cast resin platerack

Lincrusta frieze
The low-relief frieze, right, is made from lincrusta, a patented nineteenth-century type of cast plastic, which contains paraffin wax, whiting, rosin and linseed oil. It can be painted or left as it is and used successfully in most period decorating schemes.

Painted lincrusta frieze

Imitation terracotta
floor tile

Tiles and ornaments

*These plastic tiles, right,
reproduce every detail of the
material they imitate.
Decorative ornaments, like the
leaf pattern, right, and the
wreath, below, are still made
in composition by some
fibrous plaster firms, but
these imitations are in
cast plastic and can
be transformed with
special paint finishes or
gold leaf. They become
flexible when steamed,
which allows you to bend
them round curved forms.*

Plastic
anthemion

Rope decoration

*When using rope in your
decorating scheme, there is a
choice between polyester rope,
below, which looks beautiful
painted, or hemp rope, which
you can dip in plaster or
gesso (see p.32).*

White cast plastic moulding

Imitation marble
floor tile

Plastic wreath

Polyester rope
painted blue

43

SIMPLE DECORATIVE EFFECTS

The techniques in this section are mostly used for decorating large surfaces – walls, floors and woodwork, though some, such as spattering and liming, are also suitable for furniture and small areas. They are all easy to master, only slightly more advanced than painting with a flat coat of colour, and the effects are immensely satisfying. Most of the techniques involve "colour building", using a thin wash of paint or a glaze over a background colour. Colourwashing, in particular, lends itself to a wide variety of settings (there are three versions of colourwashing: one for wood and two for walls).

Examples of paint-spattered wood lie on a limed wood panel, left

One of the simplest decorative treatments for bare wood is colourwashing, above (the bottom sample has also been limed)

44

To give walls the subtlety and depth of the plaster-coloured background, and orange board, left, colourwash using similar colours

Colourwashing gives textural effects when contrasting background and wash colours are used, right

For a distressed wall finish, left, use the technique for scrubbed limewash

Three-colour colourwashing, below, lets you build rich and complex patterns

COLOURWASHING

Large decorating brush

Synthetic sponge

PVA wash

This is one of the simplest and most effective techniques for painting walls. It is descended from a long tradition of water-based-paint techniques. Instead of distemper (which was the standard paint in Europe and the USA up until the 1950s), whose poor covering qualities were often craftily disguised with decorative brushstrokes, I use a home-made PVA wash or a wash made by diluting emulsion. These water-based washes are brushed out over a white emulsion background to give smooth walls a softly patterned, subtle translucent finish. Using a slightly different colourwashing method they can be used to colour and flatter the texture of roughly plastered walls (see pp.72–73) and, in a sister technique, sponged.

TOOLS & MATERIALS

I made a PVA wash with raw sienna powder colour; I diluted it to make a pale colour for the rough wall. After using the brush to apply the wash (step 1), wipe off excess paint.

THE BASECOAT for colour-washing is white emulsion. If walls are already painted white, ensure that they are dirt-free. A wash is roughly brushed on top of the basecoat; the pattern of brushmarks is then softened with a damp brush and finally rebrushed.

Colours

Soft colours, such as dusty pink, yellow ochre, grey, raw sienna, cream and pale beige, give the most subtle results over a large area of wall space.

Stronger colours like terracotta are effective for colourwashing dados as you can see from the Venetian scheme above.

Choice of washes

You can colourwash with a home-made PVA wash (as I do here) or diluted emulsion. A PVA wash is easiest to work with because any hard lines of paint that appear when

the wash dries can be dampened with water and rebrushed. To make a PVA wash, mix water, PVA and powder colours or, for small areas, water-based tube colours (artists' acrylics or gouache); see page 157. Powder colours are highly toxic; follow the safety precautions on page 149. To give your wall a washable finish, apply a coat of matt oil-based varnish.

Using emulsion

Colourwashing with an emulsion wash gives a less dramatic finish. To make an emulsion wash, dilute emulsion 1:4 with water. Because emulsion dries to a waterproof finish, hard edges cannot be dampened and reworked. Apply the wash (*step 1*) in areas of no more than a square metre at a time and soften brushmarks (*step 2*) immediately. Practise the technique first on a piece of paper or board until you feel confident.

SPONGING

I dribbled a wall with powder colour washes and water. Once dry, I softened the dribbles with a damp sponge, below, until they became mottled, bottom.

COLOURWASHING

SMOOTH WALL

1 *Apply the wash over a dry white emulsion basecoat. Randomly brush it in all directions. (If using an emulsion wash, paint a small area.)*

2 *A few minutes later (immediately if using an emulsion wash) pass a damp brush lightly over the surface, blurring the brushmarks.*

3 *After a few minutes, when the wash starts to dry, brush with a firm pressure, lifting the remaining paint to make a patchy effect.*

ROUGH WALL

1 *For a mottled, patchy paint finish, brush on the wash in all directions, over a white emulsion basecoat. Be sure to brush plenty into the recesses.*

2 *Soften the brushmark pattern by passing a damp brush lightly over the surface; repeat five to ten minutes later, using pressure.*

3 *As this half-finished wall shows, colourwashing enhances the contrast between the raised areas and recesses of the textured plaster.*

ALTERNATIVE EFFECT

This was painted using steps 1 *and* 2 *for smooth walls. The result is a simpler-looking pattern with more obvious brushmarks and subtler colour contrasts.*

THREE-COLOUR COLOURWASHING

Incredible effects of depth and texture can be created by building up washes in three colours. Three-colour colourwashing can even produce an effect redolent of ancient watercolour-painted walls, as in the Greco-Roman Bathroom, left, where cream, yellow and green were applied to the dado. For the rich, bronze wall, I used two home-made PVA washes (one of yellow ochre and one of burnt sienna) followed by a wash of diluted cream emulsion. The first wash was applied as in steps 1–3 *for colourwashing a smooth wall (p.47); the steps opposite illustrate the application of the second and third washes.*

Burnt sienna powder colour

Yellow ochre powder colour

Cream emulsion

Decorating brush

Decorating brush

PVA

THE THREE colours used should be different but related. Choose combinations like tomato red, terracotta and beige, or blue-green, green-blue and pale blue.

The third colour is used to soften the texture and cover the surface with a translucent, mist-like layer of colour so it should be paler than the other colours. It is important to apply it sparingly with delicate brush strokes.

Paint options

I use home-made washes for the first two steps because they have greater purity and intensity of colour than ready-made paints and produce a highly textured result. The quality of colour of the final wash is not important (it should just be pale to give a dusty finish) so I use emulsion for convenience.

Powder colours are highly toxic so exercise particular caution and be sure that they do not come into contact with your skin. If you do use powder colours, follow the safety precautions on page 149.

For the softest finish, omit the PVA from the washes and varnish when dry. Or, for a finish with a slight texture dilute emulsion 1:4 with water for all three washes.

Preparation

As with simple colourwashing, this effect is suitable for smooth and rough surfaces and the best base-coat is white emulsion, applied with a paintbrush, not a roller. Rollers leave a heavy texture that becomes obvious once the wall has been colourwashed.

System of working

When you apply the second colour work on several patches of about a square metre at a time. Apply the wash (*step 1*) and rework patches that are drying (*step 2*) at about five-minute intervals.

In order to avoid making repetitive hard edges, vary the shape of the patches as you go.

TOOLS & MATERIALS

To make the first two washes mix yellow ochre and burnt sienna powder colours respectively (or water-based tube colours), water and five per cent PVA by volume (see p.157). For the third wash, dilute cream emulsion paint 1:6 with water. For an average room you will need about 1–2 litres (2–4 pints) of each. Use high-quality decorating brushes – poor quality ones shed bristles.

1 Over an already dry colourwash of yellow ochre
(follow steps 1–3 for a
smooth wall shown on
p.47), apply a wash of
burnt sienna. Brush the
paint out in a random pattern, pulling the brush in
every direction. Use a firm
pressure for this so that you
make visible brushmarks.

2 As with simple colourwashing, subtlety and
depth is created by moving
the paint about as it dries.
Use an almost dry paint-
brush and a heavy pressure
to brush over previous brushmarks, again pulling the
paint about in random directions to produce complex
patterns.

3 After some hours, when
the surface is completely
dry, apply the third, paler
wash. Brush a small quan-
tity over the surface so that it
forms a thin, smooth veil of
colour. Use a light pressure
this time so there are no
visible brushmarks.

Colourwashed stencil
Before I applied the wash of
burnt sienna (see steps 1
and 2) I stencilled this design
with gold spray paint. The
final, pale wash (see step 3)
was applied over the top.
When dry, I revealed some of
the stencil more clearly by
gently rubbing off some of the
pale wash with a rag which I
had dampened with methyl-
ated spirits beforehand.

Adding pattern
Colourwashed
walls make an effec-
tive background for
fine detail. Here, I
sprayed through a
stencil with brown
paint and added
black detail using a
fine brush.

COLOURWASHING WOOD

There is a long tradition of painting wood with water-based paints. But while applying thick layers of paint completely disguises the woodgrain beneath, colourwashing allows the natural qualities of wood to show. In this technique one or two washes of colour are brushed on to bare wood. The paint acts rather like a woodstain, in that it penetrates and colours the wood, whilst allowing the natural patterns to show. Steps 1 and 2 result in a richer finish than step 2 used alone; step 3 is used to expose more of the wood. The result of using step 2 only is shown in the flooring of the English Baroque scheme above.

Emulsion paint

Raw umber powder colour

Cloth

Decorating brush

TOOLS & MATERIALS

For step 1 mix raw umber powder colour (or artists' acrylics or gouache) with water. Powder colours are toxic so follow the precautions given on p.149. To make the wash applied in step 2 add water to your chosen colour of emulsion paint until it is as runny as milk. You need a decorating brush to apply the paints and a cloth to wipe the wood and expose the grain.

THE IDEA OF applying a water-based paint directly to bare wood floors or walls is often greeted with horror because water tends to raise the grain and can react against natural resins and oils present in wood.

But bare wood and emulsion paint are perfectly compatible because emulsion contains a poly-vinyl binder that binds paint and wood together. If the wood does become furred sand it lightly.

Preparation

Ensure that no traces of paint or varnish are left on wood that has been stripped. Wood that has been chemically stripped or bleached should be washed down with a 1:20 mixture of vinegar and water to neutralize any chemicals. (See also the information on pp.46–47.)

Choosing colours

Pale colours such as soft blue, olive green, white and pink are most compatible with the natural tones of pale wood, such as pine, and slightly stronger colours with darker woods, such as oak. Bear in mind when you choose a colour that it will look much less intense when it is diluted.

To make sure you have diluted the emulsion to the right consistency and to check the colour, test some on a small area of wood first. Left for 20 minutes, a correctly diluted wash will penetrate the wood without obliterating the grain. If necessary, alter the emulsion colour, by mixing in some water-based tube colour, such as artists' acrylics or gouache.

Varnishing

Colourwashed floors, and other areas that need to be hardwearing, should be lightly sanded, brushed with sanding sealer and then varnished. The sanding sealer prevents the varnish from soaking into the colourwashed wood and darkening it. Varnish will make the finish yellow slightly.

1 *For a subtle variation in colour start by brushing the bare wood (in the direction of the grain) with a wash of raw umber. Stir the mixture frequently to prevent the colour settling at the bottom. Leave to dry.*

2 *For a simpler finish start with this step. Using a brush, slop a generous layer of diluted emulsion on to the wood. Brush it on in the direction of the grain. Dilute emulsion penetrates and lightly stains the wood while allowing the natural grain and patterning to show through.*

3 *To expose more of the wood's grain wait 15 to 20 minutes and then wipe the surface with a clean cloth. This will remove some of the surface paint.*

Colourwashed wall, *below. Diluted emulsion was painted over stained wood and, when dry, sanded.*

SCRUBBED LIMEWASH

This technique gives walls the appearance of well-scrubbed, old-fashioned limewash (used to paint outside walls) and white distemper (used inside). I evolved the technique, which employs neither a scrubbing brush nor limewash, to give walls an aged appearance sympathetic to distressed wood and the naive wall paintings (shown below) typical of medieval interiors. But a scrubbed limewash wall finish makes an equally effective background in ethnic and country settings, like the Santa Fe Dining Room shown above.

A N UNEVEN, distressed appearance is achieved by dry-brushing a layer of water-based emulsion over an oil-based eggshell basecoat. Methylated spirits is used to rub away some of the emulsion resulting in a patchy, scrubbed-looking finish.

Applying the basecoat

Ensure walls are dirt- and grease-free before applying a coat of eggshell, diluted 1:2 with turpentine. There is no need to brush the paint to a smooth finish because only small patches of it will show. Use a neutral colour for an authentic-looking scrubbed limewash finish. I used raw sienna eggshell for the effect shown in the steps opposite; other suitable colours are mid-brown and plaster pink.

Dry-brushing

White emulsion paint is applied using a scenery painters' technique called dry-brushing. It is easy to master, but as with all techniques you are unfamiliar with, experiment on pieces of board first.

Before applying the emulsion to the wall, brush out the paint on a piece of board in order to distribute a small amount of paint evenly through the bristles.

To begin with, apply the paint with the lightest of strokes, just grazing the surface of the wall. As more paint comes off, build up the pressure until you are roughly brushing the paint with an almost dry brush.

Finishing

Emulsion paint dries to a tough finish, so most walls will need no extra protection, but in areas of high traffic, such as a hallway, you may wish to protect the paint with a coat of matt oil-based varnish.

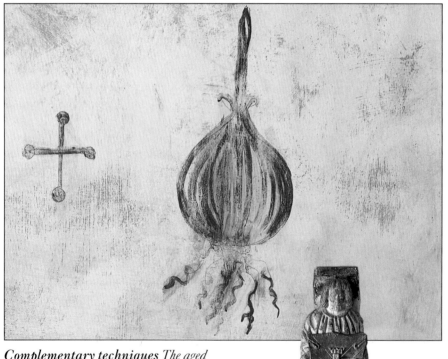

Complementary techniques *The aged finish of red-ochre wall paintings and the hand-painted knight (which I gilded and antiqued with wax) make a complementry accompaniment to scrubbed limewash walls.*

TOOLS & MATERIALS

Use a good quality decorating brush that will withstand the robust dry-brushing shown in steps 1 *and* 2 *without shedding bristles. A black hog-bristle decorating brush (shown, right) is ideal. For a room about 4m (13ft) × 5m (16ft) you may use 5 litres (1 gallon) of emulsion and 2 litres (½ gallon) of methylated spirits. The latter gives off toxic fumes so open windows and do not smoke; you can wear a respiratory mask (available from* DIY *shops).*

White emulsion

Cloth

10-cm (4-in)
decorating brush

Methylated spirits

1 *Dip the tips of a 10-cm (4-in) decorating brush in white emulsion and distribute the paint through the bristles by brushing them against a piece of board. Loosely brush the whole of the relatively dry bristle surface against the eggshell basecoat, increasing pressure to build up cloudy patches of dry-brushed paint.*

2 *When the paint has dried, patches of the basecoat will show through. If you would prefer a greater amount of texture, brush on more paint, using the same technique as above. Leave the paint to dry. For a more "brushy" effect skip this step and move straight to* step 3.

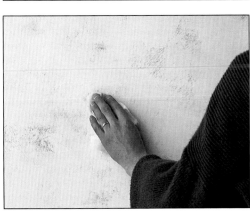

3 *Dip a cloth in methylated spirits and rub it over the whole surface. The methylated spirits will soften the dry emulsion paint, exposing the basecoat in some areas and depositing a thin white film over the whole surface. When rubbing a large area wear waterproof gloves to prevent absorption of the spirit by the skin.*

COLOURFUL ALTERNATIVE

Using two brushes, I concurrently dry-brushed indigo and purple emulsion over a pinky-brown eggshell basecoat and rubbed vigorously with methylated spirits for a highly distressed finish.

SOFTENED GLAZEWORK

Transparent oil glaze is a truly invaluable decorating material. Using the simplest of techniques, glaze tinted with artists' oil paints will cast a soft veil of colour over a painted surface, and thus impart an unsurpassable richness. Glaze can be blended and softened (see steps 1–4) to give newly painted surfaces, like the wall shown left, a warm, antique glow, add subtle depth to a painted wall, and also render colours deeper and more complex – see for example the deep-blue wall in the Medieval Bedroom scheme shown on page 100, top left. Painted mouldings, such as dado rails, and carvings, can be highlighted by stippling and wiping glaze.

TRANSPARENT oil glaze is available ready-made, or you can make your own (see the recipe on p.156). It is diluted with turpentine or white spirit to a single cream consistency and mixed with artists' oil paints to produce richly coloured mixtures that have the advantages that they do not run, like paint, or stick, like varnish.

If the diluted glaze seems too treacly when brushed on add more turpentine; if it seems too thin, thicken it with more glaze.

Glaze remains workable for at least half an hour after being brushed on and becomes fully dry within six to ten hours.

Preparation

The standard basecoat for transparent oil glaze is two smooth coats of eggshell paint, but you can also glaze over printed paper as I do in the steps opposite. The surface must be as smooth as possible because glaze will adhere to the minutest nooks and crannies, which will show up as dark marks (the only exception is antiquing, when dark marks are an asset).

Colours for antiquing

Glaze can be tinted with artists' oil paint of any colour but particular colours are used for giving surfaces an appearance of age. These include raw umber (which I used for glazing the patterned wall opposite and the corbel, far right), raw sienna, burnt umber, Vandyke brown, and any of these mixed with grey, white or black.

Varnishing and polishing

Surfaces coated with transparent oil glaze should always be varnished because glaze remains soft, even when dry, and rubs away with time.

For an exquisitely smooth finish, rub the varnished surface with beeswax on the finest grade wire wool (grade 0000). Then polish the surface to a shine with a soft duster.

Transparent oil glaze mixed with artists' oil paint

Artists' oil paints

Transparent oil glaze

Lily-bristle softener

Short-bristled decorating brush

Cloth

TOOLS & MATERIALS

You will need two decorating brushes: one for applying the glaze and one for blending it. For step 3 use a lily-bristle softener or a dusting brush. Use artists' oil paints to tint transparent oil glaze, which appears opaque until it is brushed out, when it forms a translucent film. See page 157 for tinting glaze.

1 Apply the tinted glaze with a decorating brush. At this stage do not worry if the colour is a little patchy because the glaze is rebrushed while still wet.

2 With a soft, dry decorating brush, use a light pressure to distribute the glaze evenly, softening out the brushmarks and blending in any patches of colour. As you do this the colour of the glaze will appear less intense. Finish by brushing over the surface with the lightest of strokes imaginable.

3 Using the tips of a lily-bristle softener (or dusting brush), stroke the surface of the glaze in all directions until no brushmarks are visible and the surface is faultlessly smooth.

ANTIQUE PATINA

The dusty, antique appearance of this plaster corbel was produced with transparent oil glaze and eggshell paint. First it was stippled with oil glaze tinted with raw umber artists' paint and wiped (using the technique shown below, left). Then the surface was brushed with white eggshell paint (diluted 1:4 with turpentine) and the raised areas were wiped with a cloth.

STIPPLING & WIPING

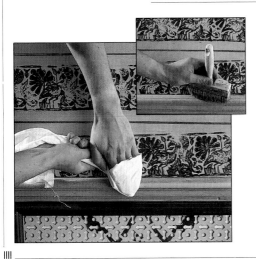

To give painted mouldings depth and shade, use the time-honoured technique of stippling and wiping. Apply the glaze. Then, holding a firm decorating brush (or stippling brush) at 90 degrees, lightly jab at the glazed surface, to produce a finely speckled impression. Wrap a cloth around your fingers and wipe the raised areas to reveal the colour beneath.

PATTERNED GLAZEWORK

Transparent oil glaze coloured with artists' oil paints has a drying time and flow properties that make it the ideal medium for brushing over a basecoat of colour and working and manipulating into broken patterns. Different effects can be produced by "dragging" a brush through wet oil glaze, gently texturing it with a sponge, bag or rag, or combing it to create patterns. These techniques are equally suitable for furniture as for large areas (the wall in the French Empire scheme, above left, was dragged).

Transparent oil glaze

Dusting brush

Decorating brush

Turpentine

Dark-blue artists' oil paint

Red universal stainer

Flogging brush

TRANSPARENT OIL glaze has the translucency, brilliance and depth of watercolour, and yet (unlike watercolour) is simple to use because it is slow-drying. It can be worked and manipulated with a brush, rag or bag for between half an hour and an hour, which gives you plenty of time to break up the surface into remarkable, delicate patterns.

Surfaces for decorating

Dragging and texturing are effective treatments for walls, doors, dados and furniture. Combing is a dramatic way of enlivening old pieces of furniture, and using a sponge instead of a plastic bag or rag (which create a lively pattern) lends a soft, muted tone to any surface, especially walls.

Choosing colours

In the French Empire Study scheme, above, I painted the wall with a basecoat of mauve eggshell paint. I then brushed on dark-blue oil glaze (see p.157 for how to mix colours with oil glaze), and dragged a flogging brush through it to expose the underlying paint. For the ragging and "bagging" technique, I used red glaze over a red basecoat.

With any of these techniques the colour combinations you choose depend largely on the mood of your room and the character of the piece you are decorating, but it is advisable to avoid glaring contrasts between the colour of the basecoat and that of the glaze.

"Bagging" *A plastic bag makes lively patterns when dabbed on wet glaze. For a more dramatic result, dampen the bag with turpentine.*

TOOLS & MATERIALS

You can buy transparent oil glaze, or make your own using the recipe on page 156. To mix it with colour (either artists' oil paint or universal stainer), see page 157. For dragging use a flogging brush or other long-haired brush. A dusting brush can be used instead of a more expensive lily-bristle softener for step 2 of ragging.

PATTERNED GLAZEWORK

1 Using a decorating brush, apply a mixture of transparent oil glaze and dark-blue artists' oil paint over an eggshell basecoat, in a thin, even layer.

2 Brush the glaze in vertical strokes with a dusting brush (or a softening brush), to soften it out and distribute it more evenly over the surface.

3 Hold a spirit level up to the wet glaze and either push the edge of it in, or score the glaze lightly with a blunt pencil, to establish vertical guidelines.

4 Following the lines, slowly drag a flogging brush or long-haired decorating brush through the glaze, holding the bristles against the surface.

COMBING

Pull a metal or rubber comb through wet glaze to make striped patterns. Cross-comb at right angles, or at very acute angles, for a pattern that resembles woodgrain.

RAGGING

1 Brush on glaze over dry eggshell paint. Dab or roll a rag (leather can also be used) through the wet glaze to make a "broken" finish.

2 Leave the glaze to dry for half an hour. Then, using just the tips of a lily-bristle softener, stroke the pattern to a soft blur.

LIMING WOOD

Limed wood has a mellow white sheen and subtle, grainy appearance that suits furniture and small objects as much as larger surfaces, like the panelling shown in this scheme, left. Liming originated in sixteenth-century Europe when furniture and panelling were cleaned and protected from worm with a caustic paste containing slaked lime. The white pigment left in the pores of the wood suggested a decorative finish and by the seventeenth century liming was in vogue – but to the horrific detriment of limers. The paste ate away their nails and fingers and the fumes dramatically reduced their life span – we are lucky to have less noxious materials around today.

Shellac sanding sealer

Stiff decorating brush and liming wax

Stiff wire brush

Soft cloth

THE MIXTURE most commonly used to lime wood is a harmless wax and pigment paste – liming wax. You can make your own from beeswax furniture polish and white pigment (see p.157) or buy it ready-made.

Preparation

Only bare wood can be limed and as preparation it should be sealed with shellac sanding sealer. Varnished or stained wood must first be stripped or bleached, washed with a 1:10 mixture of vinegar and water, sanded lightly in the direction of the grain and then sealed.

Suitability of woods

Only certain woods can be limed effectively. Open-grain woods (which have scratch-like pores in patterns that follow the grain) are the most suitable. Of these, oak, like the panels here, is the most responsive, followed by ash. Though pine is not open-grained it can be limed if you first make artificial indentations in the wood with a wire brush, using much more pressure than in *step 1*, where the oak's existing pores are simply being opened up; then follow *steps 2* and *3*. It is also possible to lime carved or distressed pine.

Beech is too hard and close-grained to prepare with a wire brush but white eggshell diluted 1:4 with methylated spirits can be washed on and then rubbed off moulded areas to create limed or pickled beech.

Alternative technique

As it is not possible to put a coat of protective varnish over liming wax, areas subject to heavy wear, such as floors and worktops, should be limed with a water and white pigment mixture (see p.157). Using this, follow *steps 1–3* and when dry, brush on another coat of shellac sanding sealer, followed, when dry, by varnish.

TOOLS & MATERIALS

Quick-drying shellac sanding sealer is used to seal the raw wood before the grain is opened with a stiff wire brush. A decorating brush is used to apply the shellac (clean the brush with methylated spirits) and the liming wax (clean the brush with turpentine). You can buy liming wax ready-made or make it yourself (see p.156). You will also need some soft cloths to remove surplus liming wax and to buff the limed surface.

1 Wire-brush the prepared wood, using a firm pressure so that you open up the grain. If you find later that you have not brushed sufficiently hard and not enough paste has taken into the wood simply brush it again. Always work in the direction of the grain; if you do not, scratches across the grain will show up white and spoil the effect.

2 Apply the liming wax with a stiff decorating brush, using a circular motion so you rub the wax into the grain; you will soon see where the open pores pick up the white wax. Work an area of about half a square metre at a time and do not worry if the effect is patchy at this stage.

3 Leave the wax for about 10 minutes so that it hardens slightly. Stretch one thickness of cloth across your fingers and polish off the surplus paste, using a circular movement. (Stretching the cloth prevents it from reaching the grain and lifting the paste out.) After 15 minutes buff with a clean cloth.

Limed pine These new pine floorboards were colourwashed (see pp.50–51) and then limed with a water and pigment mixture.

SPATTERING

With a little practice spattering is easily mastered and can be used to decorate walls, furniture and small objects with dots of paint. A loaded paintbrush is knocked against a stick to spatter furniture and other large areas. The paint flies off the brush and lands on the surface as tiny dots. The more paint that is flicked, the richer the final look, especially when more than one colour is used. The tomato-red wall of the scheme shown above, was spattered with black oil glaze and then gold paint for an exotic appearance. Paint can also be densely spattered to simulate porphyry (a purplish rock) and granite, both shown far right.

Oil-based varnish Gold paint Artists' paintbrush

Large brush

Stencilling brush

Toothbrush

Transparent oil glaze

"Spatter" stick Artists' oil paints

IN ADDITION to paint and glaze, ink and varnish can be spattered and a wide range of effects created according to the type of brush used and how heavily it is charged. Use a toothbrush or stencilling brush for small objects and thin the media you use to the consistency of milk.

For a granite effect, spatter grey, then white emulsion over a dark-grey basecoat; for porphyry, spatter purple, black, and pink paint over a rust-red basecoat.

Controlling the dots

As paint is knocked off the brush the dots become finer. Every time that you reload the brush with paint knock some off on to a rag until you get the size of dot you want. Then spatter the surface and repeat. To reduce the vibrations cover the stick with fabric.

Preparation and varnishing

Painted, unpainted, smooth and textured surfaces can be spattered.

The technique is messy so ensure you cover everything with dust sheets, and wear a mask, eye protection and, especially if you have sensitive skin, gloves. Only surfaces spattered with transparent oil glaze need be varnished. To disguise any unevenness in the finish use matt varnish; for a polished finish use gloss varnish.

"Antique" paper To give this new wallpaper an antique appearance it was glazed, spattered and given a craquelure finish (see pp.66–67).

TOOLS & MATERIALS

You need brushes (old ones that you are happy to be bashed about a bit) and a "spatter" stick (a piece of wood against which to knock the brush). To colour oil glaze mix it with artists' oil paints (see p.157). Gold paint is available from artists' suppliers. For small objects use a small brush with stiff bristles (a toothbrush is ideal) and oil-based varnish tinted with artists' oil paint (which I am using, right), ink, tinted glaze or paint (diluted if necessary).

SPATTERING

1 *Before starting, load a brush with glaze and, aiming it at a rag, flick off the excess paint. Then hold the brush parallel to the wall and hit the ferrule of the brush against the "spatter" stick. The glaze will fly off the bristles in a rain of dots. Repeat until the wall is covered with equally distributed dots; respatter any areas that are too sparsely covered with dots.*

2 *When the black glaze has dried use a smaller brush to cast a loosely distributed pattern of tiny gold paint dots. As in step 1, each time you recharge the brush, flick off the excess paint on to newspaper or a rag, before beginning to spatter the wall.*

Small-scale spattering *Dip the tips of a toothbrush or stencilling brush into tinted varnish or paint and draw your finger towards you across the brush.*

AGEING & ANTIQUING

The techniques of ageing and antiquing all produce finishes that imitate the effects of time on paint, wood, plaster, Plastic, metal and even paper. Although it may at first seem odd to want to give a worn look to fresh new paint or plasterwork, an antique finish gives a friendly, mellow feel to a decorating scheme and helps tie in new materials with the genuinely old. This section includes how to use wax or glaze to give surfaces an antique patina; how instantly to age new paintwork, plasterwork and plaster walls; and how to create a web of cracks on paintwork. The first three techniques in this section can be used independently or, for a complex effect, in the sequence in which they appear.

This new plaster casting was given an antique patina with shellac and liming wax

The resin knights were aged following the technique on pages 64–65 and antiqued with wax as on pages 68–69

Crackle varnish was used to produce the web of tiny cracks and dark-brown ink was spattered to resemble fly-spotting

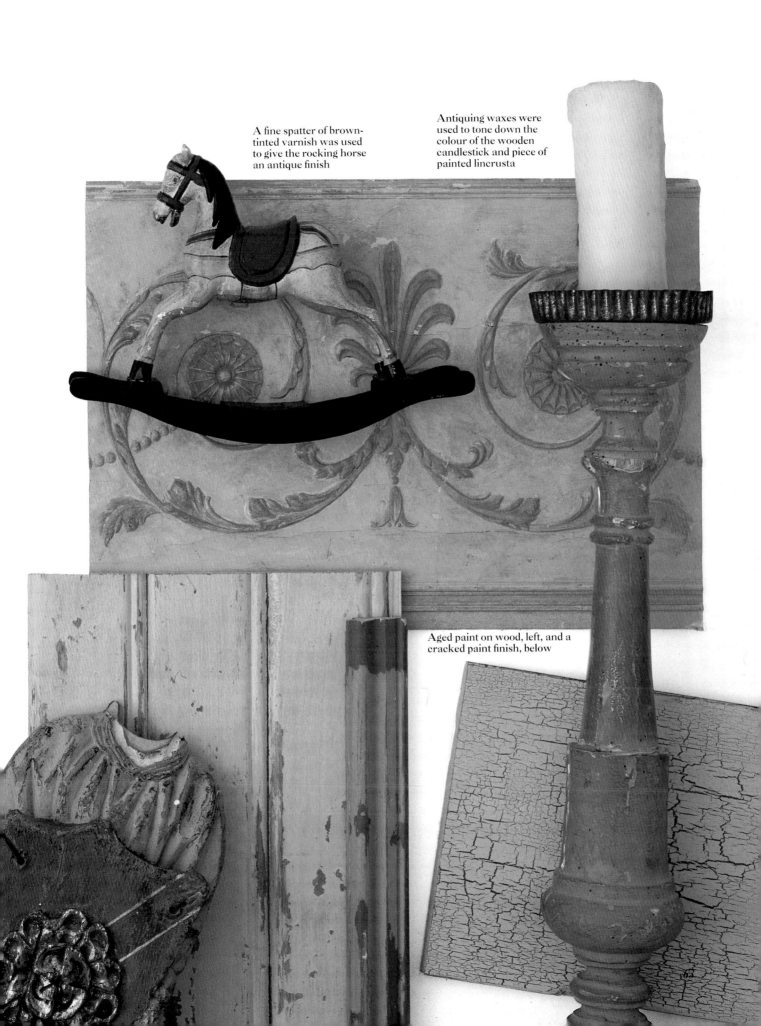

A fine spatter of brown-tinted varnish was used to give the rocking horse an antique finish

Antiquing waxes were used to tone down the colour of the wooden candlestick and piece of painted lincrusta

Aged paint on wood, left, and a cracked paint finish, below

AGEING PAINT ON WOOD

A scheme that is designed around old furniture, or combines old with new, often fails to establish a visual link between the older elements and the paint treatment of architectural features in the room, such as doors, dado rails, skirting boards and panelling. Often the sympathetic solution is to give a worn, faded look to such features (and furniture), so creating a room in which all the elements look unified. The formula for a faded look is simple: wax is used in combination with a process of building up and wearing back layers of paint. The colour combination used here is the traditional blue-green that is typically Scandinavian, but there are more vibrant alternatives (see p.21, top right).

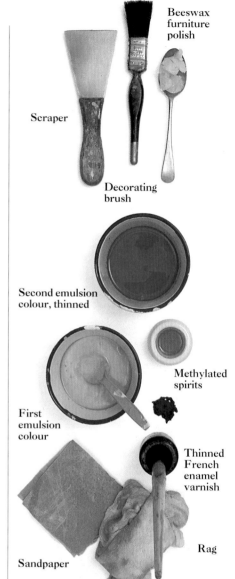

Beeswax
furniture
polish

Scraper

Decorating
brush

Second emulsion
colour, thinned

Methylated
spirits

First
emulsion
colour

Thinned
French
enamel
varnish

Sandpaper

Rag

TOOLS & MATERIALS

Use beeswax furniture polish or Copydex as the resist medium to create a chipped and peeled look, and have plenty of old rags and sandpaper (100 and 220 grit) at hand. Dilute the French enamel varnish with methylated spirits.

THE GREAT joy with this technique is that it can be applied to both new and old wood. You will, however, need to prepare wood that has already been treated: on old pine furniture, first remove any build-up of wax polish by scrubbing with turpentine or white spirit and then with a strong detergent cleaner. If the piece is varnished or painted, sand it well to remove most of the finish and key the surface. Even better, strip off the finish entirely.

Using water-based paints

The technique here uses water-based emulsion paint (rather than an oil-based paint) – not the most obvious choice for wood today, but one that is nevertheless traditional. In the past, furniture was mostly painted with water-based paints, vinegar- or beer-based washes, paints bound with casein (a latex-like milk derivative), or gesso paints (pigments bound in a chalk and glue mixture).

The complex appearance of this finish belies the simplicity of the technique and the materials used. There is no need to worry about the grain in the wood being furred or raised by the water in the emulsion paint, since the technique involves sanding at a later stage.

Finishing treatments

This technique will give the impression of wood that is chipped, peeled and faded, but to prevent any real deterioration protect the surface with varnish. Or use beeswax furniture polish, which will give the paint a sheen.

The steps opposite provide a finished treatment for wood, but you can develop the effect further by following the techniques shown on pages 66–67.

1 *Darken the wood to an aged colour with a coat of mid-brown French enamel varnish (thinned 1:2 with methylated spirits). Avoid using wood-stain as this may penetrate the paint.*

2 *Once the French enamel varnish has dried, apply blobs of beeswax polish or Copydex with a small brush. Use your little finger to elongate some of these in the direction of the woodgrain.*

3 *Leave the wax to dry for at least 12 hours before applying a liberal coat of emulsion paint. Use light pressure so you do not remove any wax.*

4 *Leave the paint to dry thoroughly – this can take up to a day when it is applied over wax or Copydex. Then apply the second colour, diluting the emulsion paint 1:3 with water.*

5 *Half an hour later you can begin to expose the layers of paint and French enamel varnish beneath. Use a scraper for obstinate blobs and a rag to remove as much of the wax or Copydex as possible.*

6 *To soften the edges, remove more paint and "tie" together the patches of exposed wood, sand carefully with 100 grit and then 220 grit sandpaper.*

SUBTLE ADDITION

You can end with step 6 or go on to create a more subtle effect by covering the whole area with a wash of the original green colour, as here (diluted 1:4 with water), or experimenting with a completely different colour.

CRAQUELURE

Most newly painted furniture and objects, mouldings and even some painted antique pieces (like the bedhead, left) can benefit from a little faded glory in the form of a craquelure (delicately cracked) finish. Craquelure was invented in eighteenth-century France, inspired by the lacquer finish of imported Oriental ceramics and Japanese Raku pottery. To enhance further the antique patina of a craquelure finish, first add softly speckled fly-spots, as I did to the wallpaper that forms the background to these pages.

Cloth

Two-part crackle varnish

Water-based ink

Cloth

Fitches

Transparent oil glaze

Terra verde artists' oil paint

Raw umber artists' oil paint

Stencilling brush

TWO VARNISHES, which are sold in a pack, interact to produce the cracks. A flexible, slow-drying varnish is applied first, followed by a brittle, quick-drying water-based one. The skill lies in judging exactly when to apply the second varnish. This should be done at a point when the first varnish is very slightly tacky. The cracks produced by the interaction of the two different varnishes are so fine that they are almost imperceptible until dirt gets into them or, in this case, a colourant, like tinted oil glaze, is rubbed into them, as shown in *steps 3* and *4* opposite.

Crackle varnish is not suitable for deeply carved surfaces because it tends to pool and will not dry at a constant rate.

TOOLS & MATERIALS

Ready-made crackle varnish comes in two bottles (see p.140). One contains an oil-based varnish (often called antiquing varnish), the other a water-based varnish. To make your own highly effective version see page 156. Mix transparent oil glaze 1:1 with earth colours (here terra verde *and raw umber) artists' oil paint to colour the cracks. Use water-based ink and a toothbrush for the fly-spot effect.*

FLY-SPOTS

1 To imitate fly-spots on a craquelure *finish (or any painted surface) spatter ink from a stencilling brush over the surface.*

2 *After two minutes dab the ink spots without smudging with an absorbent cloth to leave softly speckled rings of colour.*

1 Apply the oil-based crackle varnish with a soft brush (a fitch is ideal). Establish a really smooth, thin and even layer of varnish to ensure the drying time is constant for the whole surface. Let the varnish dry until it is slightly tacky; then follow step 2 without delay. (You might like to test the varnish's drying time before starting step 1).

2 Brush on a generous coat of the water-based varnish with a fitch. Ensure you cover the first coat of varnish entirely. Leave to dry (this should take about an hour). Cracks will appear; if necessary, you can accentuate the cracks by heating the varnish with a hairdryer.

3 To show up the cracks and antique the varnish rub coloured oil glaze all over the surface. Use your fingers or a cloth. Earth colours make the best antiquing colours for this step. I used a mixture of terra verde and raw umber artists' oil paints, but you can experiment with brighter colours.

4 Rub off most of the glaze with a cloth, taking care not to lift it from the cracks. Leave to dry for several days. The second coat of varnish is water-soluble so either protect with a coat of oil-based varnish or wipe it off with a damp sponge, so that you leave traces of colour in the cracks only.

ANTIQUING

In this process a translucent antiquing medium (either a glaze or a wax) is used to cast a spell of age on painted surfaces. Glaze or wax is coloured with a neutral, dull coloured pigment (usually brown), which represents the gradual deposit of dirt and dust on a surface that has been cherished by many years of polishing. By toning down colours and highlighting areas of wear and tear, painted wood is given the mellow beauty that occurs naturally with time. The new pine dado on the opposite page was given an aged paint finish (see pp.64–65) and then antiqued with glaze; the woodgrained panelling above was antiqued with wax.

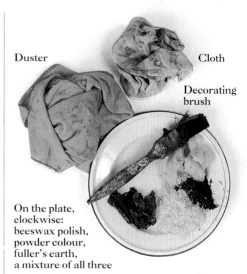

Duster · Cloth

Decorating brush

On the plate, clockwise: beeswax polish, powder colour, fuller's earth, a mixture of all three

Raw umber artists' oil paint

Transparent oil glaze

Long-bristled fitch

CONTRARY TO the usual rules of preparation, the rougher the surface, the better. This is because the antiquing medium looks most effective when it lodges in scratches, knocks and open woodgrain. If a surface is new, sand or wire-brush it, or give it a chipped or cracked appearance (pp.66–67).

To antique smooth surfaces use the softened glazework technique on pages 54–55.

Wax versus glaze

Your choice of medium will depend on the finish you prefer and practical considerations. Waxed surfaces can be polished to a shiny, antique patina. Beeswax polish can be coloured with artists' oil paints or powder colours, smells pleasant and offers some protection.

Antiquing glaze, on the other hand, gives an unsurpassable translucent finish. But it will require a protective layer on top because it does not dry very hard. For areas of high wear and tear use oil-based varnish, and for added depth of colour tint it with artists' oil paints.

Other antiquing methods

For a more opaque, dusty appearance, cover painted surfaces with a thin wash of emulsion diluted 1:4 with water, or eggshell paint diluted 1:4 with white spirit.

"Old" paint This dado was painted with blue eggshell and then diluted sage-green eggshell for an old, dusty look.

TOOLS & MATERIALS

The colours that best represent dust and dirt are raw umber and raw sienna. For antiquing glaze make a 1:8 mixture of artists' oil paint and transparent oil glaze. Add the glaze slowly to the oil paint (see p.157). For antiquing wax mix a little artists' oil paint, powder colour, and fuller's earth or powdered rottenstone with beeswax furniture polish and a little turpentine (see p.144). Powder colours are highly toxic (follow the safety advice on p.149). Use a stiff brush, such as a long-haired fitch, to fidget the antiquing medium into all of the recesses.

USING GLAZE

USING WAX

1 *Apply the antiquing glaze. Take care to brush it out in a thin layer over the whole surface as well as to work it into every crack and crevice. Use a long-bristled fitch or small decorating brush.*

2 *Delicately wipe the wet glaze. Use a circular movement and constantly reshape the cloth to present a clean surface. Your aim is to leave just a hint of colour on the surface but to leave behind the glaze in the recesses.*

1 *Brush on the antiquing wax, just as you would with the antiquing glaze, filling every recess and covering the entire surface.*

2 *After 10 minutes rub off most of the wax on the surface leaving only a thin veil behind. Take care not to disturb the wax in the recesses.*

Finishing off *To protect the glazed surface when dry, apply a layer of matt oil-based varnish or beeswax furniture polish. To antique the surface further, tint the varnish or wax with artists' oil paints before applying it.*

3 *A day later, polish the thin layer of wax remaining on the surface with a duster to give a shiny, antique patina. (This technique can be used on its own as well as over dry antiquing glaze, to add depth of colour.)*

ANTIQUING PLASTERWORK

White plaster mouldings can have a powdery and unyielding quality that cries out for a sympathetic treatment. The transformation of a fresh cornice, niche, panel, or casting like the one being antiqued opposite (which is hung as a lampshade in the Biedermeier Bathroom, left) is quick and easy. With a few simple materials you can create a delicate antique patina and a surface finish redolent of fine crystalline marble or alabaster. So good are the results that they actually encourage you to hunt out more pieces of plasterwork to transform and display on your walls as decorative artefacts in their own right.

Methylated spirits

Liming wax and decorating brush

Shellac

Fitch

Mutton cloth

Water and decorating brush

WHEN PLASTER is cast in a plaster mould, shellac is used as a mould-releasing agent. Here, it is used to add colour and textural interest to new, unpainted plaster.

How the materials work

The joy of working with the materials for this technique is their quick drying time. Shellac hardens in minutes and liming wax in half an hour. Shellac is part soluble in water so a porous surface, like plaster, that has been dampened, will absorb the shellac, to produce a soft, matt finish. If you apply a second coat of shellac a few minutes after the first one (see *step 2*) it will dry to give a strongly-coloured surface gloss.

Technique options

Shellac comes in colours ranging from brown to orange. Alternatively use French enamel varnish (see p.141), or tint liming wax with artists' oil paint.

Plaster that has been painted must be stripped before using the technique shown here. This is time-consuming but you can instead work on top of emulsion paint to create a finish that is similar to the one here. Mix a 1:2 solution of shellac and methylated spirits and apply sparingly, as in *step 2*. Follow *steps 3* and *4* but do not expect to create the same lustre and depth of colour.

Transforming plaster *Follow* steps 1–4 *to give new white plaster, left, the mellow sheen of antique plaster, right.*

TOOLS & MATERIALS

Liming wax can be bought ready-made or you can make your own (see p.156). Shellac comes in several grades; choose a treacly brown one and dilute it 1:1 with methylated spirits to make it more workable and a little paler. Apply the shellac with a pointed brush such as a fitch (see p.124).

1 Unless your plaster is very fresh, and therefore very damp, you must wet it to prime the surface for the shellac. Soak the plaster by brushing water over it several times – it is amazing how quickly the water is absorbed. For a cornice, treat one whole side of the room at a time; remember to protect the room with plastic sheeting.

2 While the plaster is still damp use a stiff-bristled brush to stipple and fidget the dilute shellac into the carving (avoid using broad strokes, as these will show up later). Apply one coat for a mottled, matt surface and a second, a few minutes later, if you want a richer, glossier colour.

3 Leave the shellac to dry for about 10 minutes and then work in the liming wax. Make sure you penetrate every nook and cranny, otherwise you will have ugly, dark "holes" in the finish. Keep the coverage of wax even by transferring any excess on the brush to new areas, or diluting the mixture on the surface with turpentine.

4 Immediately, take an absorbent rag, such as mutton cloth, and rub the raised areas of the moulding to take off some of the wax and reveal the shellac beneath. Where there are expanses of plain surface, use the cloth to dab a pattern into the wax, taking most of the wax off. Leave to dry for at least half an hour before polishing to a sheen.

AGEING PLASTER WALLS

Although it may seem slightly perverse to want to damage and distress a perfectly smooth, flat wall, the effect can be charming, adding texture and character to a room. The crumbly plaster wall of the Australian-style balcony, left, gives a sense of decayed grandeur, which is perfect for the setting. (See also the French Medieval Bedroom on p.100 and the Venetian Studio on p.46.) If your home is not blessed with the texture of decay then consider using this technique to introduce it as a theatrical gesture in a dining room, bedroom or hallway.

THIS TECHNIQUE uses wax in a "resist" method similar to that used on pages 64–65. Wax that has been heated is applied in patches before plastering, preventing adhesion of the plaster coat. The dry plaster can then be chipped away in random-looking crumbly shapes.

Wall preparation

Plaster can be applied to an unpainted or painted plaster wall. The colour of the paint will show through the chipped areas, so for a neutral effect paint the wall the same colour as the plaster. Before you brush on the wax, coat the wall with PVA mixed 1:1 with water.

Choice of plaster

For this technique use white gypsum (finishing coat) plaster. Its advantages are that its setting time is slower than other plasters and, being white, it can be tinted with powder colour when being mixed (see p.157) or colourwashed when dry (see pp.46–49). Mix up the plaster with water according to the manufacturer's instructions and add one per cent PVA – this will help the plaster adhere to the surface.

Applying plaster

The plaster coat need only be a few millimetres thick and so it is relatively easy to apply. If you have ever tried plastering you will know how difficult it is to achieve a really flat surface free of bumps and pits. The joy of this technique is that blemishes actually contribute to the finish. The trick when using a trowel is to keep it angled slightly off the surface so that only the trailing edge touches as you move it.

Alternative finish

Instead of plaster you can use a PVA-bound, smooth-texture coating (available from DIY stores). This is much easier to work with than decorator's gypsum plaster. Use a brush to apply it and then smooth it with a trowel when it is nearly dry. This smooth-texture coating will peel rather than chip away when dry, giving a slightly less ragged texture.

Hammer

Mallet

Trowel

White gypsum plaster powder

Plaster mixture

Shellac

Beeswax polish mixed with turpentine

Water

PVA

TOOLS & MATERIALS

PVA is used to seal and protect the surface, and one per cent by volume should be mixed with gypsum finishing plaster and water. The trowel is used for plastering; if you are plastering large areas you may also want to invest in a hawk (a hand-held tray for the mixed plaster). It is advisable to wear eye protection for step 5 as plaster can fly off the surface in all directions.

1 Seal the surface with PVA mixed 1:1 with water and allow it to dry. I started with a coloured background but this is not essential.

2 Gently heat equal quantities of beeswax polish and turpentine in a bain-marie; brush on the cooled mixture in random patches.

3 While the wax is still soft, trowel on the plaster in broad, arc-like movements, until the whole surface is covered with a thin layer.

4 Once the plaster has begun to set, splash plenty of clean water on it with a brush and remove ridges and obvious marks with a wetted trowel.

5 Leave the plaster to dry for a day. Then knock the wall with a hammer or mallet to loosen the plaster over the waxed areas, and scrape this away.

6 Sand the surface lightly to soften the edges and remove any unwanted tool marks. Apply a protective coat of PVA diluted 1:4 with water.

FAUX EFFECTS

False, or faux effects transform the appearance of a surface and so deceive the eye into thinking that it is something else. The techniques for creating the effects of stone, marble, wood, rust, gold and even leather are all given in this section, together with ideas on where to apply them. As well as "tying in" ordinary materials, like plastic and hardboard, with a rich decorative scheme, faux finishes can be used to provide rooms with an unexpected element, such as walls with a dark lead finish, or skirting boards that look like dusty terracotta.

Metal leaf, shown on a wood moulding and plastic ornament, can be laid haphazardly to reveal the colour of underlying paint

Sand is used to give *faux* rust, below, a gritty texture

An example of a stone finish executed in emulsion, above, and woodgraining done using a simple home-made wash, left

These hardboard shapes with a leather-like texture in unusual colours can be seen as wall panels on page 80, top left

The yellow Siena marble, below, and the brown fossilstone marble, bottom, are sophisticated finishes

Plastic ornament with plaster finish

The effects of terracotta, above, and verdigris, right, are achieved by the accurate representation of colour and the random building of layers

PIETRA SERENA

There is nothing to equal the texture of stone for adding power and weight to an interior. But it is not necessary to have the real thing – it can be convincingly imitated on all kinds of materials, including wood, plastic and plaster (see the Florentine-style room, left, for example). The type of stone imitated here, is pietra serena, *which is rough-cut marble that over the years turns from grey to a mellow, raw-umber brown. Once the main building material for the great Renaissance buildings of Florence, its distinctive colour (which is often copied by decorators for exterior stucco and stonework) can add Italian panache and historical significance to interior schemes.*

Diluted white emulsion and swordliner

Methylated spirits

Texturing paste

Eggshell basecoat and decorating brush

Decorating brush

Whiting

Rag

TOOLS & MATERIALS

Eggshell paint is used for the basecoat and emulsion diluted with water for the veined lines. The texturing paste is made from emulsion paint and whiting; add whiting until the mixture begins to look bitty and solid, like congealed butter icing (you should be able to make it peak). Use a decorating brush to apply the basecoat and the paste and a swordliner or lining brush (see p.124) for the veining.

THE characteristics of this stone – its mellow colour, varied texture and pale veining – can be simulated using simple materials.

To reproduce the colour of *pietra serena* start with a dark, grey-brown eggshell basecoat. If you cannot find a suitable colour add dark-grey eggshell paint slowly to umber-brown eggshell paint (if you do this the other way around you will end up with a colour that is too cold and blue). Eggshell paint can be applied to most surfaces, provided they are correctly primed (see the section on surfaces on pp.30–43). Eliminate any surface texture before you apply the primer.

Stone texture

To imitate the stone's worn and textured surface, start by applying a thick layer of a paste made from pale grey emulsion paint and whiting. Once dry, rub with methylated spirits. This slightly softens some of the roughest areas of paste and completely removes others to reveal patches of the smooth eggshell basecoat, which resemble the exposed or raised parts of stone that have become highly polished through wear. Finally, add thin lines to imitate the white veining characteristic of the stone. Protect the finished surface with a coat of matt, oil-based varnish.

Imitating limestone *Follow* steps 1–4, *but use a creamy-beige texturing paste for a limestone colour.*

1 Apply a thick layer of texturing paste over the dark, grey-brown eggshell basecoat. Pull the brush away from the paste sharply to create a stippled texture with little peaks. Leave the paste to dry – this may take up to two days in damp conditions.

2 Dip a rag into methlyated spirits. With the rag in a tight bundle, rub the surface firmly, using a circular motion. The methylated spirits will soften the peaks of the paste to resemble worn, rough-cut stone. In places it will also expose the smooth grey-brown eggshell basecoat.

3 Draw a swordliner (or a lining brush) across the surface to create fine, fractured veins. Use white emulsion, diluted 1:1 with water.

4 The swordliner will naturally deposit small puddles of paint in some areas; immediately blot some of these with your finger. Blot others when they are half dry, to leave rings and outlines of white paint. This occasional softening of the line will make it appear as if it runs right through the depth of the stone.

SANDSTONE

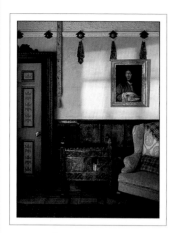

This technique follows in the eighteenth-century tradition of using paint to imitate exterior finishes indoors. But whereas early methods were aimed at suggesting materials such as sandstone in the enormous hallways and echoing stairwells of grand homes, this technique results in a more subtle finish that will withstand close scrutiny in rooms of a modest size. The result of the steps opposite is a dusty and granular finish that both looks and feels like the material it apes. I used this technique for the wall in the Scottish setting shown above. Not only is the effect fun to produce but the theatrical result will add atmosphere.

FIRST PAINT the wall with a basecoat of white emulsion. If it is already painted white, ensure that it is clean and that none of the paint is flaking.

If you are applying a new basecoat you can brush on the paint in a reasonably rough-and-ready manner because most of it will be obscured by the emulsion paint and glaze applied in *steps 2* and *3*.

Texture and colour

Like the leather effect on pages 80–81, the sandstone effect is created by building up texture with thick layers of paint. The texture is "heightened" with coloured transparent oil glaze.

Diluted eggshell paint is used to add a thin veil of colour that tones down the previous colours and makes the effect more realistic. The surface is then lightly sanded so that some of all the colours beneath are exposed.

Protection

The diluted eggshell paint applied in *step 4* will protect the oil glaze beneath and this is suitably durable for most rooms. However, in a hallway, for example, you may wish to protect it with matt varnish.

Special tips

Stipple on a very thick layer of the emulsion paint (*step 2*). If the surface does not look textured enough, stipple the paint again five minutes later. Rather than stipple the whole wall at once, stipple each stone-shaped area separately; this way each stone will have a slightly different character.

Include one or two curved as opposed to right-angled corners of mortar but avoid having too many or the wall might look like something from a Walt Disney cartoon.

Sandstone and mortar *This "sandstone" wall is as subtle and realistic when viewed from nearby as from afar. Emulsion paint was used for the lines of mortar.*

Large
decorating
brush

Pale-beige emulsion

Diluted white
eggshell paint

Flat fitch

Burnt umber artists'
oil paint

Transparent
oil glaze

Small
decorating
brush

100 grit
sandpaper

Cloth

TOOLS & MATERIALS

The tools you need are two decorating brushes (one large, one small), a flat fitch (or similar-shaped artists' brush), a cloth and 100 grit sandpaper. Mix the transparent oil glaze with brown artists' oil paint (see p.157 for instructions) and dilute white eggshell with a little turpentine. You can experiment with applying more than one colour of emulsion in step 2 *for different effects.*

1 *Draw irregular stone shapes on a dry, white emulsion basecoat; leave space between the stone shapes in which to paint in the mortar (*step 6*).*

2 *Use a large, stiff-bristled decorating brush to stipple on the pale-beige emulsion paint. Paint almost up to the pencil lines.*

3 *When dry, brush on transparent oil glaze mixed with brown artists' oil paint. Wait five minutes. Then wipe the glaze with a cloth.*

4 *After the glaze has dried (this may take a day), apply diluted white eggshell. Brush it out to make a thin, even layer of colour and leave for a day.*

5 *When the paint is dry, sand the whole area with 100 grit sandpaper. This will reveal the pale-beige emulsion applied in* step 2.

6 *Following the gaps between the "stones", use pale-grey emulsion and a fitch to paint freehand the mortar lines between each of the individual rectangles of "sandstone".*

LEATHER

The rich, textural quality of medieval worked leather adds theatrical grandeur to a room. The techniques for faux *leather can achieve the same sumptuous effect, as shown on the right, as well as the more subtle leather effect on the blue and pink wall panels of the Tudor decoration, shown in this scheme, left. The technique was developed from an accidental discovery made by a pupil of mine when learning how to antique a textured paint surface. Rather than brushing on the paint she "fidgeted" it, making swirling patterns which revealed themselves when antiqued (steps 3–5). Adapted and refined, this provided a starting point for an effective imitative finish.*

Raw umber oil paint

Burnt sienna oil paint

Decorating brush

Sandpaper

Transparent oil glaze

Cloth

THE TECHNIQUES of leather finishing can be applied to any clean and grease-free surface. Both the finishes here are suitable for walls and furniture.

"Stamped leather"

An obelisk-shaped mask was used to make the "leather" on the opposite page look as if it has been stamped. (The same mask was used in a different technique for the frieze in the Tudor scheme above.) To pattern leather, make a card shape. Use it to make a guide for painting and to shield the first colour of emulsion (*step 1*) from the second, in which the brush is "fidgeted" to make swirling, leathery patterns.

Your choice of colours can vary according to how fantastic you want the leather to look. To convey a realistic sense of the material use light tan, and brown emulsion paints, together with a mixture of raw umber and burnt umber or burnt sienna artists' oil paints to colour the transparent oil glaze.

For leather with no "stamped" pattern follow *steps 1–5* opposite, without using a mask, painting and texturing the whole surface.

Subtle effects

The softer finish of the Tudor panels shown in the period reception room above, was achieved by applying brown artists' oil paint mixed with glaze over pink and blue emulsion basecoats, textured as in *step 2*.

Finishing touches

Either finish can be left semi-matt or, for a sheen, rubbed with beeswax furniture polish. Protect surfaces with semi-matt varnish.

Making a mask This mask was cut from oiled manila card (see pp.130–31).

TOOLS & MATERIALS

Use a small decorating brush to apply the two shades of emulsion paint. The paint must be thick enough to allow you to build texture into it. If you think the paint will fall back on itself mix in a little whiting. Mix a little raw umber and burnt sienna artists' oil paint 1:1 with transparent oil glaze. Some artists' oil paints are toxic and can be absorbed through the skin, so should be applied with gloves if you are working on a large area (see the table on pp.148–51). Use cartridge paper or the back of a piece of sandpaper for step 5.

1 *Loosely draw round the mask; remove it and stipple the outlined area with tan emulsion to make a peaked texture. Leave to dry for a day.*

2 *Secure the mask in its original position. Apply a thick layer of brown emulsion, "fidgeting" the brush all over the surface around the mask.*

3 *Remove the mask and leave the paint to dry for a day. Then rub artists' oil paints mixed 1:1 with transparent oil glaze over the surface.*

4 *Using a cloth, gently wipe off the glossy excess of the glaze mixture, leaving the rest in the recesses of the textured emulsion.*

5 *To reveal patches of the emulsion colours beneath, gently rub the raised areas (including the obelisk shape) with the back of a piece of sandpaper.*

6 *The obelisk shape, which was not painted with the brown emulsion in step 2 will appear lighter. To give the shape a sharper outline draw round it with a pencil.*

TERRACOTTA, PLASTER & LEAD

The weathered patina of old lead, the salty bloom of terracotta and the dusty surface of raw pink plaster have something in common. They are all mineral finishes that result from chemical changes on raw materials, and they can all be imitated with a brush, a sponge and emulsion paint. The simple and quick technique shown opposite is for a terracotta finish; just use different colours of emulsion paint to imitate plaster and lead.

Synthetic sponge

Terracotta emulsion

Caramel-brown emulsion

Cream emulsion

Large fitch

Short-bristled decorating brush

Decorating brush

THIS TECHNIQUE relies for its effect on broad, random marks made with a sponge and paintbrush, so it is only effective on fairly large surfaces. The odd run of paint is part of the effect, so work on vertical surfaces or objects that you can turn upright.

The wall and skirting board in the scheme above, and the large frame, far right, have a terracotta finish; see below right for the plaster-effect finish and below left for lead. Terracotta, plaster and lead all have a dry dustiness that can only be imitated with water-based paints such as emulsion, which dry to a matt finish.

Areas prone to scuffing, such as a hallway dado, or water splashes, such as a bathroom wall, should be protected with one coat of oil-based extra matt varnish or matt acrylic varnish. Do not use gloss varnish because it will destroy the required dusty effect.

TOOLS & MATERIALS

You can use a decorating brush of any quality for brushing on the basecoat and the paint in step 1, *as any faint brush-marks will be disguised by the subsequent sponge marks. Natural sponges have the best configuration of holes but an excellent alternative is a synthetic sponge, ripped to give it a random shape. Use emulsion paint, diluting it as indicated in the steps opposite.*

LEAD & PLASTER

Lead effect *Apply dark-grey emulsion, skip* step 1 *and follow* steps 2–4, *using light-grey paint.*

Plaster effect *Follow* steps 1–4, *simply substituting a pinky-brown colour for the terracotta paint.*

1 Brush on terracotta emulsion (diluted 1:1 with water) over a dry base-coat of caramel emulsion. Keep brushing the paint (even as it dries) to leave a soft and patchy layer, allowing cloudy patches of basecoat to show through here and there. For a plaster effect, use pinky-brown emulsion diluted 1:1 with water.

2 When the paint is com-pletely dry (one to five hours later) use a clean dec-orating brush to dampen the surface (this makes the paint applied and sponged in the next steps more workable). Dampen areas of a square metre at a time. For plaster and lead, dampen the pinky-brown or dark-grey paint.

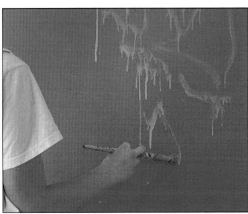

3 Apply cream emulsion (diluted 1:2 with water) with a large fitch or 2.5-cm (1-in) decorating brush to make a random pattern of blobs and lines; use enough paint for it to run slightly. Follow this step, using the same colour for plaster, and light grey for lead.

4 Dab and smudge the blobs and lines with a slightly damp sponge. The thin film of water on the wall (applied in step 2) will cause the sponge marks to soften into gentle blurs and the paint to run. At intervals of about a minute, sponge the area for 10–15 seconds; con-tinue this until the sponge marks become clearer.

THE EFFECT
You can clearly see how the water applied in step 2 causes the sponge marks to blend into a wispy blur and how the odd run of paint is allowed to remain after being sponged as in step 4.

VERDIGRIS

Patinated metals have a rich variety of colours and textures that are fascinating reminders of the passage of time and the action of the elements. Verdigris, with its green, crumbly saltiness, is the result of naturally-occurring corrosion and affects brass, copper and bronze. The decorative appeal of verdigris is such, that metalworkers reproduce it with acids and heat in a highly toxic process. You can create authentic-looking verdigris – safely – using simple materials and following the steps shown opposite. The brand-new metalwork in the bathroom, above, was transformed using this technique.

Whiting

Verdigris paste, ready to apply

Pale-blue emulsion

Artists' paint-brush

Mint-green emulsion

Diluted deep blue-green emulsion

French enamel varnish

Methylated spirits

Yellow-ochre spray paint

THIS technique is suitable for any metal or plastic surface that you can work on horizontally. The verdigris paste will not adhere to vertical surfaces but you can produce a verdigris effect (like the wall on p.102 and the background here) using a slightly different method, which is shown below.

Application

If you are not working on bronze, copper or brass you can create a suitable base colour by painting your surface with bronze powder colour or spray paint (use gold for a brighter effect). If your surface is silver, like the metalwork here, simply paint it with brown French enamel varnish (see p.141).

Like marbling, woodgraining, and ageing and antiquing paint-work, the aim of this technique is to imitate a naturally-occurring phenomenon and to trick the eye into believing that no human hand has had any part in the process.

This depends on achieving a random effect. Apply all the layers on top of the first coat of paint (thick pastes, spray paint and powder) in random patches rather than even layers so as to achieve a natural-looking result. You can seal the powdery finish with diluted PVA, followed by matt varnish to produce a hardwearing surface.

Vertical surfaces *To verdigris vertical surfaces apply diluted emulsion paint in the colours of verdigris and flood water through the damp paint layers.*

TOOLS & MATERIALS

You need two verdigris pastes, one that is pale blue and one that is mint-green. To make verdigris paste make a 1:2 mixture of methylated spirits and emulsion paint, then sieve in whiting until the mixture is the consistency of butter icing. Methylated spirits evaporates quickly, so you may need to add more as you go along to keep the mixture workable.

1 Brush a 1:4 mixture of deep blue-green emulsion paint and water over the bronze- or gold-coloured basecoat and leave to dry.

2 Work the pale-blue and the mint-green verdigris pastes over the surface together. Vary the thickness and texture to create a random effect.

3 Whilst the verdigris pastes are drying, use a yellow-ochre spray paint to apply small, light patches of colour haphazardly across the surface.

4 Flood the surface with water to expose the underlying colours. Just let the water wash over the top of the mixture – do not work it in.

5 Take some whiting or plaster powder and lightly sprinkle it across the surface, pressing it into the damp and sticky mixture. Pay special attention to recesses.

6 When the mixture is half dry, wipe some – not all – of the raised areas with a rough cloth to expose patches of underlying colour. When dry, seal with diluted PVA.

IRON & RUST

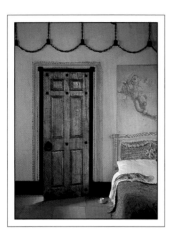

Metal finishes can be exploited to great decorative effect in an interior scheme. In the Spanish Baroque Bedroom, shown left, the wooden door, treated to resemble iron, has a silvery metallic sheen, lightly dribbled with rust. On the skirting board, architrave and door studs, metal is imitated in its more heavily corroded state as dark rust. Both of these simple techniques are demonstrated here, and they can be applied to any surface.

THESE SIMPLE metal techniques use materials that are built up in separate layers to give naturalistic metallic finishes. In the rust technique, see *steps 1–4* below left, a wood surface is given texture with a mixture of glue and sand. This will also cover any imperfections on the surface. The final coat is French enamel varnish (see *step 3*), mixed with methylated spirits and highlighted with emulsion paint. In the iron process, diluted black emulsion is applied over a dry coat of oil-based paint.

Random effects

The success of these metal finishes depends on the randomness of the surface pattern. In the final stages, water is used to break up the basecoat of paint on the "iron" door, and, in the rust technique, methylated spirits is applied on the varnish, to emulate the texture of metal. To "randomize", when using rags and brushes, constantly change the angle at which you hold them, the direction in which you work, and the pressure you apply.

Protecting the "metal"

Although the rust effect is very durable (the glue, sand and paint form a sort of cement), it is still worthwhile protecting it with a coat of matt oil-based varnish. This will give the surface a really hard finish.

The silver metallic paint used for the iron technique contains metal powders. These are likely to be aluminium, in which case no protection is needed. But sometimes paints contain other metals; the air causes these to darken and they need protection. Check the ingredients of your silver paint, and if you are unsure whether it contains aluminium, protect it with semi-matt polyurethane varnish.

IMITATING RUST

1 *Coat the surface generously with undiluted PVA and throw sand at it. On vertical pieces hold a board beneath to catch the excess.*

2 *Leave to dry thoroughly and brush on deep brown emulsion, fidgeting the brush to work the paint well into the texture of the sand.*

3 *When dry, brush on a coat of rich brown French enamel varnish, diluted 1: with methylated spirits.*

4 *After 10 minutes brush on methylated spirits and touches of rust-coloured emulsion. Make patterns with more methylated spirits.*

TOOLS & MATERIALS

Basic tools – decorating brushes, a dusting brush, an artists' brush and a cloth – are needed for imitating iron and rust. The brown emulsion is used for the rust, and the brighter, rust-coloured emulsion is used for highlights in both of the finishes. Methylated spirits is used to work on the paint and French enamel varnish, in the technique on the left, producing random patches, which suggest the texture of rust.

French enamel varnish

Cloth dipped in black emulsion

Decorating brush

Decorating brush

Brown emulsion

Methylated spirits

Artists' brush

PVA

Rust-coloured emulsion

Sand

Dusting brush

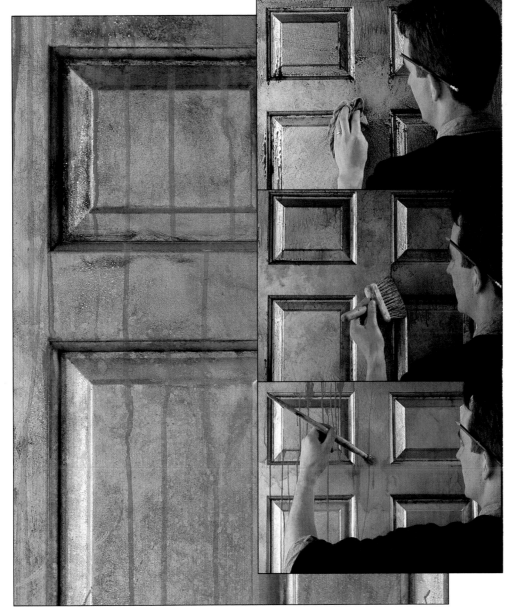

IMITATING IRON

1 *Paint the surface with silver metallic paint. Dilute black emulsion 1:4 with water and add a drop of detergent. Apply with a damp cloth to produce random patterns. The mixture dries fast so cover only a small area of the surface at a time.*

2 *As the mixture dries, soften it with a dry dusting brush, or a lily-bristle softener, to make the marks of the cloth less obvious. Soften out the paint more in some areas than others, to lend a ran-domness to the texture.*

3 *When thoroughly dry, brush water over the surface and dribble rust-coloured emulsion (diluted 1:2 with water) through it. The water brushed on the surface will dilute the "rust" further, making it dry pale and translucent over the silver as the large example on the left shows.*

CARRARA & SERPENTINE MARBLE

The decorative technique of simulating marble dates back to Roman times and there is a wealth of different styles. White Carrara and green serpentine marble are quite easy to paint and can be applied successfully to different surfaces, from floors and skirting boards to small objects. Painted well, marble adds style and a certain classic quality to a room, as can be seen in the Florentine Hallway, shown above left.

Transparent oil glaze

Black artists' oil paint

Tissue paper

Decorating brush

Terra verde artists' oil paint

Swordliner

Small artists' brush

Dusting brush

Turpentine   Lily-bristle softening brush

FOR CENTURIES marbling was carried out in distempers and gesso paints. But the nineteenth century saw a desire for a new realism and in Britain the new and cheap medium adopted was transparent oil glaze, which was used as a vehicle to extend expensive artists' oil paints.

Transparent oil glaze is still used for marbling today. Buy it ready-made or follow the recipe on page 156 to make your own.

The best surface preparation for transparent oil glaze is two coats of white eggshell paint. This gives a degree of slip whilst presenting a reasonably smooth surface. Oil glaze rubs away with time so always coat with semi-gloss varnish when dry and wax for a reflective sheen.

Oil glaze attracts dust like a magnet so work in a draught-free area and vacuum it before you begin. Always shake your brushes free of dust before using them.

TOOLS & MATERIALS

Use artists' oil paints to colour transparent oil glaze (for mixing instructions turn to p.157). Black is used to tint the glaze for Carrara marbling, terra verde and white for the first serpentine glaze and terra verde only for the second. Artists' oil colours are toxic so always clean your hands after using them. For information on dusting and softening brushes see pages 126–27 and for the swordliner, turn to page 124.

Marbled floor *I used a combination of different coloured marbles to make a striking pattern; the method for the yellow marble is overleaf.*

CARRARA MARBLING

1 *Using a soft cloth, rub some transparent oil glaze into the eggshell background to give the surface a greater degree of "slip".*

2 *Dip a thin brush in black-coloured glaze and use it to paint a few very rough veins on the surface, adding the occasional dot and spatter.*

3 *Using a dusting brush or softening brush, stroke at the veins with the tips of the bristles, to spread them slightly in all directions.*

4 *Dip a swordliner in turpentine and use it to paint the odd wet line over the glazed surface, following some of the softened veins.*

5 *Soften the surface again, brushing the wet lines made in* step 4 *in one direction only, to make feathery crack-shaped veins.*

6 *Stroke the surface in all directions with the tips of a lily-bristle softener, to eliminate all brushmarks and create a hazy blur.*

SERPENTINE MARBLING

1 *Brush on a glaze coloured with* terra verde *artists' oil paint. Dab at the surface with a pleated piece of tissue paper to add pattern.*

2 *Leave the surface to dry for at least a day and then thinly brush on a much deeper* terra-verde *coloured glaze over the entire area.*

3 *Dab the surface with tissue paper as before, ensuring you present a clean surface to the wet glaze each time. Vary the pressure you use.*

SIENA MARBLE

Although simply executed marbles, such as Carrara and serpentine, convey a cool, elegant beauty, the most effective use of marbling with paint is to divide a surface up realistically into blocks and inlays, and incorporate small amounts of rich and complex marble in a design, as in the marbled and varnished flooring shown on page 88. Siena marble has long been favoured by Italian masons for this type of decoration as it possesses a strong concentration of colour and pattern, and might look too intense and overpowering over a large area. As well as decorating floors, Siena marble can be used in patterns on box lids or table tops.

Dusting brush

Soft cloth

Lily-bristle softener

Pencil badger-hair softener

Artists' paint brush

Artists' oil paints

Transparent oil glaze

Black wax crayon

Sword-liner

Natural sponge

Turpentine

THE TECHNIQUE for Siena marble is more time-consuming than other marbles, but it pays dividends when you see the final results. Study original examples or pictures of Siena marble – the more you notice about it the more life-like your copy will be.

Preparing and varnishing

As a marble finish should be faultlessly smooth, sand down your surface if necessary and paint it with two coats of cream eggshell. Oil glaze attracts dust so clean and vacuum the day before you start. Ensure brushes are dust-free and do not wear wool clothes. When the glaze is completely dry, protect it with a coat of hard varnish, otherwise it will gradually wear away.

Making patterns

Use masking tape as an aid to marbling neat shapes. Stick on the tape before painting with the cream eggshell and remove it while this is still wet, carefully wiping off any glaze overspill with a cloth as you work.

If the colour of Siena marble does not appeal use the same technique but a different coloured glaze, a sumptuous red or emerald green, for example. For Brescia marble (which forms part of the marbled floor on p.88) mix a browny-red glaze.

Veins *The distinctive black veins of Siena marble are drawn with a black wax crayon dipped in turpentine.*

TOOLS & MATERIALS

Buy or make some transparent oil glaze (see p.156). Mix the glaze with a little raw sienna artists' oil paint (see p.157). As some artists' oil colours are toxic, always clean your hands after using them, and make sure there are no paint deposits under your nails. A fine artists' brush can be used instead of a swordliner, and an artists' sable brush instead of a badger-hair softener. For information on brushes see pages 122–27. Turpentine or white spirit can be used for step 4.

1 *Wipe a layer of transparent oil glaze over the surface. Then dab on patches and streaks of raw-sienna coloured oil glaze.*

2 *Roughly soften the patches and streaks with a dusting brush, pulling the glaze across the surface in all directions as you do so.*

3 *Using a softener, stroke the patches with the tips of the bristles, to remove any brushmarks and soften the glaze further.*

4 *Dip a swordliner or fine artists' brush into turpentine and then use it to paint a few wet veins across the surface of the glaze.*

5 *While the veins are opening up, use a sponge to dab some turpentine very sparingly on the surface. This will create a mottled effect.*

6 *To prevent the turpentine from opening up the glaze further, dab the sponged areas with a cloth, or soften or stipple them with a brush.*

7 *Dip a black wax crayon into some turpentine to soften it and then use it to draw a few veins in the wet glaze in "boulder and pebble" formations, which are typical of the marble.*

8 *Let the surface dry for about 10 minutes, by which time the turpentine will begin to evaporate. Then gently soften the veining with a badger-hair softener or sable artists' brush.*

9 *Using a soft cloth, dab and blur some of the black veining so that it "recedes" into the stone, and wipe out some of the "boulders and pebbles" to make cream-coloured stone chips.*

FOSSILSTONE MARBLE

Some of the most effective mineral finishes are those created when a brush hardly touches the surface, and all the pattern is created in a random fashion by mixing different media. Fossilstone marble is an excellent example of this type of decorative finish and the results are quite beautiful, as can be seen in the decoration here. If possible, lay the surface to be decorated flat on the floor so that the solvent can form pools (for vertical surfaces, see below). Use either a water-based wash as I did, or an oil-based glaze.

PVA

Burnt sienna wash

Raw umber wash

Fitch

Methylated spirits

Lily-bristle softener

Decorating brush

FOR MARBLING to look real, it requires the smoothest possible basecoat. Sand the surface if necessary and apply two coats of pale-beige eggshell paint, taking care to avoid visible brushmarks.

Media

The traditional medium for marbling is oil paint, or coloured oil glaze. However, for fossilstone marble, nothing beats the variety of patterns obtainable with a home-made water-based wash. This is made from powder colour, water and a little PVA, which is added to bind the mixture.

Before applying the wash add a drop of detergent; this prevents it from opening into patches when applied over the basecoat.

Drying times

In *steps 2* and *4* the wash is manipulated whilst drying. The difficulty with using a water-based wash is that it dries so quickly (10 minutes on a warm, dry day) that only areas under one square metre can be tackled at a time. Oil-based glazes take upwards of two hours to dry.

If you are concerned that you may not be able to work fast enough use an oil-based glaze – the results are good but not as spectacular. To tint the glaze, mix transparent oil glaze with raw umber artists' oil paint (see p.157).

Both PVA water-based washes and oil-based glazes remain soft when dry, and so you will need to protect them with a coat of oil-based varnish.

Vertical surfaces Follow steps 1–4, *using a sponge instead of a brush to apply the methylated spirits, water and coloured wash in* step 3.

TOOLS & MATERIALS

To make the water-based washes, slowly add 0.5 litre (1 pint) of water mixed with 1 tablespoon of PVA to 2 tablespoons of powder colour (mixed with a little water), stirring all the time. Add a drop of detergent. If the colour does not look right add more powder colour or more water and PVA. Powder colours are highly toxic; follow the safety precautions on page 149. Protect your eyes with goggles when spattering with methylated spirits as in step 3.

1 *If you are using a water-based wash, rub a small amount of fuller's earth into the dry eggshell basecoat to absorb any grease. Brush the raw umber wash on in criss-cross strokes, covering under one square metre; continue with steps 2–4 and then start on a new area. If using oil glaze, cover the whole surface in one go.*

2 *Using a decorating brush, roughly stipple the surface to break up the coarse pattern of brush-marks. Work quickly if you are using a water-based wash; the advantage of oil-based glazes is that they give you much more time to complete this step.*

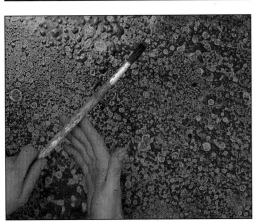

3 *This is the magical part. Spatter methylated spirits on to the water-based wash to make it split. Then flick on a little water here and there to make rivulets and pools of liquid, and (this is optional) spatter on spots of the burnt sienna wash. The overall effect should be random. (On oil-based glaze, use turpentine and then methylated spirits.)*

4 *Allow the surface to dry partially so that only the pools and rivulets remain wet (you can speed up the drying process of oil glaze with a hairdryer). Then, using a lily-bristle softener or dusting brush, soften these wet areas, stroking away the brushmarks and carrying the wet, coloured liquid over the surface in all directions.*

CLAIR BOIS

This easy and effective technique for a clair bois *(pale wood) finish is the first to experiment with when learning to woodgrain. Using a simple home-made wash and a flogging brush you can convey the impression of the fine, polished finish of pale woods (such as maple and satinwood) on surfaces ranging from inexpensive wood furniture and doors, to dados and floors. Biedermeier-style furniture is traditionally made from pale woods so this technique is particularly suitable for a Biedermeier-style room scheme (above); I used it to decorate the exterior of a bath and then protected the wash from water with a coat of varnish.*

Water-based
wash brushed out

Small
decorating
brush

Water-based wash

Raw sienna
powder colour

Flogging brush

TOOLS & MATERIALS

Water and raw sienna pigment in the form of powder colour are needed for the wash (see p.157). If you are covering a small area, you may wish to use gouache instead of powder colours. (If you use powders follow the precautions on p.149). A flogging brush provides the best clair bois *finish.*

THE WATER-BASED wash used here dries quickly and can be brushed into feather-edged forms and crisp shapes. Surprisingly, it is easier to work with this than the oil-based glaze (used for the woodgraining techniques shown on pp.96–99) and it can be dampened and reworked after it has dried. If you can work quickly enough, you may be able to complete all the steps before the wash dries. If not, work on just one area at a time, swapping between *steps 1* and *2.* Alternatively, work on the whole area at once, brushing any of the wash that has dried with a little water to make it workable again.

Choice of finish

Steps 1–2 for a burr wood finish create a pattern that looks like a knotted wood veneer (see the close-up on the top half of the page and the "Biedermeier" bath). A subtler effect can be created by applying less pressure on the brush. A grainy effect can be achieved by following *steps 1–2* for an elongated grain (shown on the bottom half of the page).

Preparation

The smoother the surface you are going to give a *clair bois* finish, the better. As preparation, carefully apply two coats of cream eggshell paint. When dry, rub the surface with a little whiting or fuller's earth to absorb any surface grease.

Finishing touches

When the glaze has dried apply a coat of oil-based varnish. Brush it on swiftly and lightly so as not to disturb the pigment in the glaze. I use goldsize (see p.140), which is quick-drying or, where necessary, a tough oil-based varnish.

To give the "wood" a shiny and smooth finish redolent of French polish follow this decorator's trick: when the varnish is completely dry polish it first with beeswax furniture polish on some grade 0000 wire wool, and then with a duster.

BURR WOOD FINISH

1 Apply the glaze with a decorating brush. It does not matter what brushmarks you leave as long as the whole surface is covered with an even layer of wash. The wash dries within minutes; if it dries before you move on to step 2 dampen it with a wet paintbrush.

2 Hold a flogging brush at 90 degrees to the surface and firmly push the bristles into the wet wash. The long bristles will "splay" outwards, making wild, knotty shapes, which look like the burr patterns of some wood veneers. For a more subtle effect and texture repeat with a lighter pressure.

ELONGATED GRAIN

1 Push a flogging brush through the wash, so the bristles splay outwards. This will give the effect of a very coarse but lively woodgrain. Work fast so you can go on to step 2 before the wash starts to dry. If the wash does dry dampen it with a wet brush.

2 Hold a flogging brush flat against the surface and pat the wash while pulling the brush towards you. This softens the wilder patterns made in step 1.

OAK GRAIN

Apply the wash as in step 1 shown below. Soften out the brushmarks with a softening brush, and run a checking roller charged with black paint over the surface (see p.128).

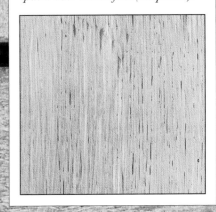

GRAINING WITH A BRUSH

Woodgraining is the technique used to imitate the beautiful, random patterns of natural woodgrains. It reached the height of sophistication in the nineteenth century, when highly skilled artists emulated every known configuration of woodgrain. The comparatively simple technique opposite, is for a non-specific but effective woodgrain finish shown on the door of the Scottish Sitting Room, above. See pages 98–99 for a more pine-like woodgrain and pages 94–95 for a clair bois *(pale wood) finish.*

ANY SMOOTH surface that can be painted with eggshell paint can be woodgrained. Standard modern doors, like the ones here, can be transformed to blend in with a room's decoration and expensive dark woods, like mahogany, can be imitated on inexpensive woods and those that come from renewable resources (see pp.34–35).

Other suitable candidates for woodgraining include skirting boards, furniture and floors.

Glaze and surface preparation

For woodgraining I use transparent oil glaze, coloured with artists' oil paints and diluted to a single cream consistency with turpentine (see p.157 for tinting glaze). Glaze does not form a hard, protective surface so varnish over the top.

Prepare the surface for woodgraining by applying two coats of eggshell paint. This provides a smooth working surface.

Woodgrain colours

The final wood colour results from the colour of the eggshell basecoat and the colour of the glaze. For the door shown on the opposite page, I used glaze tinted with burnt umber artists' oil paint, over two different eggshell basecoats (brown and soft yellow) to give the impression of two sorts of wood.

For different-coloured woodgrains, experiment with other colours of eggshell paint and glaze mixed with any of the earth-colour artists' oil paints.

Transforming a door *This once green door was sanded down and painted with eggshell basecoats of ochre-cream and pink. Once grained (using the glaze colour and technique shown in* steps 1–6), *the panels were stencilled with emulsion and outlined in black.*

Dusting brush

Flogging brush

Transparent oil glaze mixed with burnt umber artists' oil paint

Transparent oil glaze

Cloth

TOOLS & MATERIALS

Any clean decorating brush can be used to apply the tinted glaze. You also need a flogging brush, the long hairs of which can be pushed, pulled and patted in the glaze. Use a dusting brush to soften the glaze. (For specialist decorating tools see pp.128–29.)

1 *Brush a coat of glaze on to the panel mouldings. Then jab the glaze with a flogging brush to create a random woodgrain pattern.*

2 *Apply glaze to the panels, and push the flogging brush upwards, to produce the whorls and scratches typical of woodgrain.*

3 *Wipe away any odd marks with a cloth. Then lay the flogging brush almost flat against the surface and pat it to soften the previous marks.*

4 *Push the flogging brush through the glaze on the door frame (as in step 2). On narrow areas use the edge of the brush.*

5 *Using the flat side of the flogging brush, gently pat the glaze as in step 3. Take care to work the brush slowly towards you.*

6 *If you want a subtle effect wait 10 minutes and then stroke the glaze in the direction of the grain with the tips of a dusting brush.*

GRAINING WITH A ROCKER

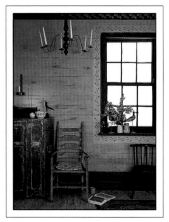

If you are wary of attempting woodgraining because you feel it may be too complicated, try your hand at this simple technique that uses a little-known "wonder" tool, called the rocker. It creates pine-like patterns and is particularly effective if used in small quantities in a room, on doors, for example, or skirting boards, as in the New England Living Room scheme shown above. For a realistic-looking woodgrain use only natural colours over wood or a painted wood-coloured background. Fantasy variations using unnaturalistic colours also look effective; I have seen old farmhouse beams with rough-and-ready blue and red graining that gave them an original and naive charm.

T HE WORKING surface of the rubber rocker is curved and ribbed in semicircles to make the woodgrain pattern. The medium I use is artists' oil paint, either thinned with a little turpentine (for an intense pattern), or mixed with transparent oil glaze (for the subtle effects shown here).

For faultless graining the paint or glaze should be applied to a smooth, non-absorbent surface. Any bumps will interfere with the pattern, which is only an advantage if you want a rough-and-ready effect. When the paint or glaze is dry (this takes a day or two) apply a coat of oil-based varnish.

Dusting brush

Decorating brush

Woody-coloured artists' oil paints

Rubber rocker

USING A ROCKER

Hold the rocker so that the curved surface is touching the wet glaze or paint and then pull the rocker gently towards you, slowly altering the angle you hold it at as you go (left to right, above). As the rocker moves, its sections of ribbing scoop up the glaze, as in step 3 opposite.

TOOLS & MATERIALS

A rubber rocker is indispensable for this technique. Although virtually any brushes can be used to apply the glaze and soften the pattern, I prefer to use a dusting brush for the latter job, because its bristles are strong enough to work with the sticky glaze, while the bristle tips are fine and soft. Experiment with woody-coloured artists' oil paints, such as raw umber or raw sienna, mixing them 1:3 with transparent oil glaze and a spot of turpentine (see p.157) or, for a bolder pattern, diluting them with just a few drops of turpentine.

1 *Using a small decorating brush, paint the glaze over the surface, brushing it out to make an even layer. On pitted surfaces or on grooved surfaces like the matchboarding here, push the glaze into the crevices because it is better for the overall effect that these show up later as dark rather than light.*

2 *Decide on which direction you want the wood-grain to go and, using a dusting brush, gently brush the glaze layer in that direction, using just the tips of the bristles. Aim for a soft, overall grainy look at this stage.*

3 *Take the rocker and pull it slowly through the glaze, as described on the opposite page. Keep changing its angle as you pull it along, but do not jerk it or rock it too wildly as movements like these will leave unpleasant marks. Clean the rocker repeatedly with a rag to prevent a build-up of glaze in the rocker's grooves.*

4 *Soften the grain pattern with a dusting brush to blend it into the background and remove any thick deposits of glaze that the rocker may have left. Drag the brush through the glaze for a "pulled" look (as I am doing), or open up the glaze by patting the surface with the flat side of a flogging brush (shown on p.129) to create oak-like pore marks.*

GILDING – METAL LEAF

Gold has a magical, seductive quality, reflecting colours of intense warmth and variety. For centuries, water-gilders have practised the highly skilled art of laying loose sheets of gold over layers of damp glue. But there is a much simpler, quicker method, known as transfer gilding, which is illustrated here. Transfer gold leaf (which comes on waxed tissue paper) is laid on top of water-based goldsize. The transfer leaf can be applied directly on to any hard surface including wood and sealed plaster, or, for a silky-smooth finish, over gesso. The three celestial shapes, far right, were gilded directly on to painted plaster.

GILDING WITH transfer leaf (either real gold or inexpensive Dutch metal leaf) gives a richer and more lustrous finish than gold paint or metallic powders. Once you are confident of gilding flat surfaces, move on to carved mouldings and accessories, such as lamp bases. New gilding can be antiqued (see p.102).

Optional gesso preparation

For a perfect, silky-smooth finish, gild over gesso, which is a thick, tough paste that is applied in layers. On a flat surface, the slightly convex shape formed by gesso makes gold leaf look even more reflective and shimmering.

Gesso comes in various forms but rabbit-skin and PVA versions are easy to scrape and polish (*step 2*, far right). To highlight any eventual holes and imperfections rub with fuller's earth; then sand and polish further. Gesso dust may cause asthma so always wear a mask when sanding large areas.

In imitation of the coloured clays sometimes used under gilding, use ready-coloured gesso, colour your own with powder colours, or paint dry gesso with gouache.

Technique tips

Transfer leaf sticks to grease, so before starting clean your hands and rub around the area to be gilded with whiting.

The key to a smooth finish is to lay the leaf when the goldsize is tacky, usually after about half an hour. Water-based goldsize will remain tacky, ready to accept the leaf, for many hours; for this reason, it is easier to work with than oil goldsize, which varies in drying time from brand to brand.

Finishing

Dutch metal leaf oxidizes and in time turns black. To prevent this, brush with goldsize several days after gilding, by which time the underlying shellac will be dry. Real gold leaf needs no protection.

APPLYING TRANSFER LEAF

1 *Draw the outline of the design; you may like to use a cutout as a guide. Paint on goldsize (tinted with artists' gouache paint so that it is visible).*

2 *When the goldsize is almost dry but slightly tacky, gently press on a sheet of transfer leaf (I am using Dutch metal). Carefully peel away the tissue.*

3 *Several hours later gently rub off the loose leaf with a soft cloth or cotton wool. Then polish the gilded area with a cloth.*

Ready-made rabbit-skin gesso

Artists' paintbrush

Water-based goldsize

Dutch metal leaf

Shellac

Artists' oil paint

Soft cloth

TOOLS & MATERIALS

Goldsize is the adhesive for transfer leaf. The traditional type of gesso (used here) is made from rabbit-skin glue. It is gently heated in a bain-marie *(double boiler) and applied warm. To make your own traditional gesso or a modern PVA version, see page 156. Gilding materials are covered in detail on pages 146–47.*

GESSO PREPARATION

1 *Paint on three or four layers of gesso until the surface is slightly raised. If you are using rabbit-skin gesso, leave to harden overnight after the last coat.*

2 *When the gesso is dry, scrape with a craft knife and polish with silicone carbide paper and grade 0000 wire wool until the finish is smooth.*

3 *Apply one coat of coloured gesso or gouache. Let it dry and then polish to a shine with grade 0000 wire wool. This step is optional.*

4 *To gild over the gesso, apply leaf as shown, left. The gesso provides a build-up of relief which makes the gold glow even more brightly.*

GILDING – METALLIC POWDER

Shimmering and brilliant, the effects that can be achieved with metallic powder are superior to those of gold paint, and from a distance much decorative work in metallic powder is mistaken for gold leaf. Gilding with powders is inexpensive and quicker than gilding with metal leaf, making it suitable for small and fairly large areas, like the Art Nouveau frieze here. For added drama, metallic powder can be patinated (see pp.104–105).

Duster

Dusting brush

Camel-hair mop

Mask

Metallic powder

French enamel varnish

Artists' oil paint

Artist's paint-brush

Oil goldsize

Cloth

Soft brush

METALLIC POWDERS are available in many colours, including the gold used here. The powder is brushed or shaken on to a surface coated with a thin layer of goldsize. As metallic powders are highly toxic they should not be inhaled. It is important to wear a mask over your nose and mouth, and goggles over your eyes. Ventilate the room when applying the goldsize but not when handling the powder.

The only requirement for gilding with powders is that the surface is reasonably smooth and non-absorbent. Absorbent surfaces, such as bare wood and plaster, should first be primed with paint or sealed with sanding sealer.

Protective coating

Leave the gilded surface to dry for three days before applying white polish or shellac (see pp.140–41) diluted 1:1 with methylated spirits.

ANTIQUING GOLD

1 To antique metallic powder or gold leaf liberally brush with French enamel varnish (diluted 1:1 with methylated spirits).

2 Dab off some of the French enamel varnish to reveal the gold beneath. Alternatively, spatter with more varnish (see p.60).

TOOLS & MATERIALS

The drying time of oil goldsize ranges from one to twelve hours (see Technique tips on p.100). Apply the metallic powder with a pad of cotton wool, a camel-hair mop or soft make-up brush (see specialist brushes on p.128). For antiquing use French enamel varnish (a shellac-based varnish) diluted with methylated spirits.

1 *Tint some goldsize (you may prefer to use water-based goldsize as featured on pp.100–101) by mixing in a little artists' oil paint; this will enable you to see where you have brushed it. Using a soft brush apply the goldsize, brushing it out into a thin, even layer. Wait until the goldsize is nearly dry but still tacky.*

2 *Protect your mouth and nose with a mask and your eyes with goggles. Dip a camel-hair mop (or make-up brush) into a small pot of metallic powder. Shake off excess powder, inside the jar, and then gently stroke the tacky goldsize with the brush to leave a thin layer of metallic powder.*

3 *Leave the goldsize to dry completely hard (preferably wait for 24 hours). Wearing a paper mask and goggles, dust off any loose powder with a dry dusting brush; vacuum up the loose powder. Gently polish the gilded area with a soft cloth or cotton wool until it is really gleaming.*

"Gold" ornament *Gilding with metallic powder is a quick and inexpensive way of transforming an ornament, like this plastic leaf, into a rich, lustrous decoration. Follow the steps shown above using gold, bronze or silver metallic powder.*

103

PATINATED GOLD

This technique is used to give surfaces that are painted gold, or gilded with metal leaf or powder, added decorative interest in the form of a dramatically patinated finish. (It can even be used directly on cast metals.) The complex appearance of the patina belies the simplicity of the technique. French enamel varnish, methylated spirits and spray paint are built up in opaque and translucent layers of colour. The technique is suitable for surfaces that can be worked on horizontally, ranging from furniture to mouldings, like the gold-sprayed skirting board and the hardboard frieze above. The frieze was given extra pattern with colours sprayed around a triangular template.

Diluted French enamel varnish

Methylated spirits

Gold spray paint

Pointed fitches

French enamel varnish

HISTORICALLY, a variety of methods have been used to patinate metals. Today, chemical patination is the most common process but it is highly toxic and ineffective on real gold.

The technique here is much safer and, used over copper-coloured paint, gives surfaces the appearance of antique bronze. To give gold leaf or metallic powder a more subtle antique patina use the simple method shown on page 102.

Importance of varnishing

On exposure to air any metal finish, other than pure gold, will become dull. It is, therefore, important to protect the finish with a coat of oil-based varnish. This also serves to harden the rather brittle French enamel varnish, which is used as part of the technique.

Do not use an alcohol-based varnish (consult pp.154–55) as this will dissolve the methylated spirits used to dilute the French enamel varnish (which is applied in *steps 2* and *3*), and the whole effect will be ruined.

Alternative materials

French enamel varnish is available from specialist suppliers. If you are unable to obtain it, make some from woodstain and white polish, using the recipe on page 156.

Alternatively, colour oil-based varnish with artists' oil paints and dilute it 1:1 with white spirit. Using this mixture, follow the steps opposite, substituting turpentine for methylated spirits.

Safety advice

When you spatter the methylated spirits (or turpentine) in *step 3* protect your eyes from splashes with a pair of goggles. The fumes of methylated spirits are narcotic and sometimes stimulate reactions in asthmatics; if you use it in any quantity wear gloves and a respiratory mask as well as goggles.

TOOLS & MATERIALS

French enamel varnish is available from specialist suppliers (see p.164); if you find it difficult to obtain, follow the recipe on page 156. Ready-made French enamel varnish should be diluted 1:1 with methylated spirits. You need three to four different colours, including at least two shades of brown. Have two pointed fitches (or pointed artists' brushes) to hand: one for applying the French enamel varnish, the other for the methylated spirits.

1 Dilute several colours of French enamel varnish with methylated spirits. Apply each colour, daubing some in loose patches and spattering others by knocking the loaded brush against your fingers. (The technique of spattering is shown in detail on pp.60–61).

2 Dip a clean brush into methylated spirits (this will dissolve the French enamel varnish) and work it among the patches of colour, joining some of them up and completely covering others (to make them almost translucent). Work quickly and make as random an effect as possible. Leave for five minutes to allow the methylated spirits to evaporate.

3 Take a little undiluted French enamel varnish on the brush and gently knock it against your fingers to spatter the whole surface with little dots of colour. Try to distribute the dots evenly. Then spatter the surface with methylated spirits in the same way. This will dissolve some of the varnish, breaking it into a variety of complex pool-like patterns.

4 Lightly spray the surface with gold paint, applying it just here and there, where the methylated spirits is still wet. The paint and methylated spirits will react to make a broken pattern. This softens the effect, so you may wish to omit this step if you are working over a background of gold leaf, which is more reflective and lustrous than gold paint.

STAINED GLASS

Though the true art of stained glass is not a very complicated one, it does require specialist training and equipment. This lively theatrical imitation, on the other hand, can be done simply, and apart from the fact that it scratches easily, it is almost indistinguishable from the real thing. Imitation stained glass is achieved by painting coloured varnishes on glass and then sticking on lead strips. The stained glass in the steps opposite was based on a Charles Rennie Mackintosh design. This, together with the window design, above, was taken from a furniture inlay detail.

Small artists' brush

Black marker pen

Long-bristled fitch

French enamel varnish

Methylated spirits

Self-adhesive lead in two widths

FRENCH ENAMEL varnish, the medium used to paint the glass, is available from specialist suppliers, in a range of colours. To make any colour subtler, dilute the varnish with methylated spirits, but avoid mixing different colours together – the resulting combinations often turn out to be rather dull and muddy.

Useful tips

To help the varnish stick to the glass, clean the glass thoroughly with methylated spirits before beginning painting. Try to avoid getting the varnish on your skin because the dyes stain heavily. French enamel varnish becomes brittle when dry, and will scratch and wear away easily, so you may wish to protect your design by covering it with another sheet of glass, or perspex. It is also a good idea to use this decorative technique in areas that are out of reach of small children.

Decorative uses

It is easy to get carried away and overdo things with this technique, thus spoiling the effect, so be judicious. Stained glass works best in discreet quantities, for example on glass panels over a door, on skylights or on mirrors, rather than decorating every window! Abstract designs or patterns are generally much easier to produce than naturalistic ones.

Design ideas *All kinds of contrasting sources (not just stained glass designs) can provide inspiration; this is a medieval tile pattern.*

TOOLS & MATERIALS

Soft, pliable brushes (long-bristled fitches, for example) are essential for this technique, plus some small artists' brushes. French enamel varnish is the colouring medium (see p.156 to make your own). Methylated spirits, which is used to dilute the French enamel varnish brushed on in step 1, and is applied in step 2, should always be used in a well-ventilated area. Self-adhesive lead is obtainable from DIY stores. Lead is poisonous so keep your fingers away from your mouth after handling it and wash your hands.

1 Draw out your design on tracing paper, then tape this on to the reverse side of the glass. As an extra guide, trace the outline of the design on to the front of the glass with a black marker pen. Using a very soft brush (I am using a long-bristled fitch), paint on the French enamel varnish (diluted 1:1 with methylated spirits).

2 Since French enamel varnish quickly dries to a transparent finish, obvious brushstrokes are usually difficult to avoid. To disguise them and make a decorative mottled pattern, dab a small artists' brush dipped in methylated spirits over the surface. This dissolves the varnish even when it is dry, creating rings and patterns.

3 Using undiluted black French enamel varnish and another small artists' brush, paint in any details on the design, like the veining on the leaves, here. You can also use undiluted varnish to outline any parts of the design that are too small to outline with lead.

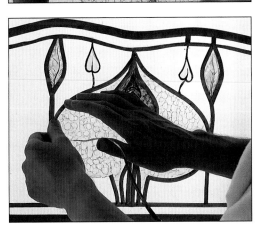

4 When the varnish is dry, carefully press some self-adhesive lead around your design. Stretch it around shallow curves and, to make it fit around tight bends, snip little cuts into the inside edge of the lead with heavy-duty scissors. The lead will hide the black guidelines drawn in marker pen.

PAINTED PATTERN

Although there is no quick method for transforming the decorator into a fine artist with a practised eye, there are a number of straightforward and highly effective techniques you can employ to create painted patterns, and these are explained in this section. Stencilling is perhaps the most versatile of such techniques, and even the simplest design can be treated to look like the freehand work of an artist.

Découpage, the old tradition of pasting up cut out engravings, was my model for hand-colouring photocopies, which can be used for occasional interest or as part of a grander scheme. Finally, come the sister techniques of grisaille *and* trompe l'oeil, *which will set you on the path to more ambitious illusionism.*

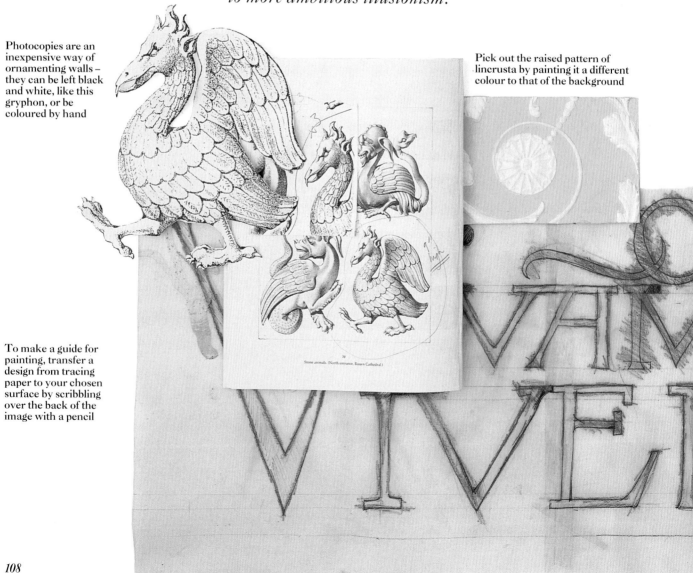

Photocopies are an inexpensive way of ornamenting walls – they can be left black and white, like this gryphon, or be coloured by hand

Pick out the raised pattern of lincrusta by painting it a different colour to that of the background

To make a guide for painting, transfer a design from tracing paper to your chosen surface by scribbling over the back of the image with a pencil

Different stencil effects can be created with spray paints, below left, and by stippling with a brush, below

Use colour photocopies for highly detailed colour imagery, especially for repeat patterns

Applying a complex stencil to a patterned surface creates the impression of painstaking freehand work

An intricate floral stencil, below

Painted ornament and mural

MAKING STENCILS

Designing and making your own stencils can be an exciting and very rewarding process. Although it may take some time and considerable patience, you will achieve real pride and satisfaction as you see your design take shape. The blue stencil-led wall in the scheme, on the left, is an example of the designs it is possible to create. Of course, you need not start with anything quite so ambitious – try a fairly simplified design to begin with and then progress from there. Once you have mastered the technique, you will be limited only by your imagination.

For centuries, stencils have been cut from either brass or tin plate, or, more commonly, made out of stencil card, which you can still buy today from artists' suppliers. It is made from stout manila card soaked in either shellac or linseed oil. (To make your own, see p.156.)

Once you have cut out your stencil, spray both sides lightly with spray paint. This will prevent the card from curling when you use it with water-based paints.

Islands and bridges

The art of making a complicated pattern lies in how you "bridge" the various parts of the pattern together. Floating "islands" of card in the middle of a cut area need to be tied across to the edges to hold the stencil in one piece.

The bridges should occur at regular intervals otherwise the stencil will fall apart. With practice you can incorporate these bridges into the design of the stencil. In a delicate pattern try to make the bridges fairly thin. Most simple patterns, like the fish design on page 115, need no bridges at all.

If you have cut out a particularly intricate pattern, glue a sheet of fine dressmakers' netting on to the back of the stencil. This will also help to hold the stencil together when you are using it. Use waterproof masking tape to repair stencils that become damaged.

Reference materials The stencil design shown in the steps opposite was taken from this book on nineteenth-century ornament (you can see the area of the design enlarged). Patterned papers and fabrics are also a rich source of ideas.

TOOLS & MATERIALS

The essential tool for cutting out is patience, plus a sharp craft knife. If you use a scalpel, do not apply too much pressure as the blade might snap and fly off. If you plan to do a lot of cutting, consider investing in a cutting mat.

VISUALIZING THE PATTERN

Here you can see the pattern (top) that a stencil design (bottom) makes when it is painted. It is always worth checking the results of your stencil on a piece of paper before you actually begin decorating.

1 Draw a grid over the original design, and number and letter the horizontal and vertical axes. (If you are taking a design from fabric, draw or photocopy it for this step.) Decide what size stencil you want and draw up a new grid on tracing paper. Copy the original design, square for square, on to the tracing paper.

2 Turn the tracing over and tape it on to the stencil card. Pencil over the reverse of the outline, pressing down firmly. This will transfer the original tracing you made in soft pencil on to the card. (A short cut to steps 1 and 2 is to copy the design using an enlarging photocopier, then glue the copy directly on to the card and cut out the design.)

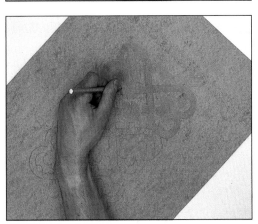

3 It is a good idea to colour in your design on the card at this stage to give an idea of what it will look like as a solid pattern. With a coloured pencil, draw in a system of bridges to link up any floating islands of card in the middle of the design. These bridges will also serve to strengthen the stencil.

4 Cut out the coloured parts of the stencil, taking care not to cut through any bridges. Do take your time when cutting, as it pays to be accurate and you run less risk of cutting yourself. If you do make a mistake or tear the card, stick it back together with masking tape.

USING STENCILS

Stencilling is one of the most effective and inexpensive ways of adding pattern and ornament to a room. It is also one of the simplest – paint is stippled through a manila card stencil (see the tools and materials on pp.130–31) to create an image with a charming softness that manufactured borders and wallpapers cannot imitate. The fleurs-de-lys *here, were stencilled on the rough plaster wall of the French kitchen scheme shown above. Add freehand details, as I have done, to make your stencils look like impressive pieces of freehand painting, lightly sand them for a faded look or blend them into the background with a thin wash of paint.*

Diluted emulsion and sable artists' brush

Emulsion and stiff decorating brush

TOOLS & MATERIALS

Use a stiff decorating brush or a stencilling brush for stencilling and a sable artists' brush or lining brush for painting freehand detail.

SPECIAL EFFECTS

The plaster wall, top, was stencilled as in steps 1–4 *and then painted with diluted emulsion; the small fleur-de-lys, above, was stencilled on a panel, which was then limed (see pp.58–59).*

M Y STANDARD stencilling paint is emulsion because it comes in a wide range of colours, dries fast and can be used on many surfaces (see the table on pp.152–55). Other types of paint, including spray paint, can also be used for stencilling; the effects are shown overleaf.

You only need a little paint on your brush, so before starting, dab off any excess on to waste paper. To add freehand details use a sable artists' brush or lining brush and diluted emulsion (this flows on easily). For the medieval *fleurs-de-lys* designs here, I used two typically medieval colours: deep apple green and russet.

Combination techniques

The stencils were lightly sanded to give them the same aged, faded quality as the cracked plaster wall. Sanding is also an effective way of giving stencils on wood the same rough graininess as their background and stencils on a sponged or colourwashed background a similar soft unevenness. To blend a stencil even more closely with its background, paint over both with a thin wash of diluted emulsion, as I have done, above right.

Stencilling can also be combined with the technique of liming wood. The design, right, was stencilled on to a panel, which was then rubbed with liming wax.

Patterns and repeats

If you are using your stencil to make a border, frieze or regular pattern, measure up and mark the position for each image. If you skip this step you may find that images are slightly out of line, meet badly at the corners of a room or are chopped in half where they meet the ceiling. Use a spirit level for accurate horizontal alignment and a plumb line for vertical alignment.

1 Work out where you want each stencil and mark the position lightly with a pencil. Use a long ruler for measuring, a spirit level for horizontal alignment and a plumb line for vertical alignment.

2 Secure the stencil with low-tack masking tape and/or low-tack adhesive spray. Put a little emulsion paint on the brush (dab off any excess before starting) and stipple it on with a quick, dabbing action. Use a stiff decorating brush (I am using one here) or a stencilling brush.

3 When the paint has dried, remove the stencil. For outlining and adding detail use a sable artists' brush (as I am) or a long-haired lining brush, and emulsion paint diluted 1:1 with water so that it flows off the brush easily.

4 To age and fade the newly stencilled image (shown in the inset), wait for the paint to dry and then lightly sand it with 100 grit sandpaper. This produces pleasing results on textured surfaces such as plaster and bare wood and smooth surfaces that have been sponged or colourwashed (see pp.46–51) and have soft variations of colour.

113

STENCIL EFFECTS

Decorative borders of stencilled patterns on a plain background have become a familiar sight in homes, restaurants and hotels. But many people are unaware of the wide variety of effects that can be achieved with stencils and their versatility as a decorating aid. The secret is to think of a card stencil not simply as a decorative emblem to be transferred to a surface, but as an elementary template to be used to complement and elaborate other special paint techniques. The pattern of the stencil itself may be extremely intricate and original and executed in unusual colours, or it may be used in subtle and interesting ways, perhaps on a patterned or perforated background.

THE SIMPLEST use of stencils is to repeat them to form a running border. For a more complex effect the stencil pattern can be overlapped and the position of the stencil shifted slightly each time (see the oak leaf stencil on p.115). Some all-over designs can even be made into excellent "wallpaper", such as the intricate stencilling on page 110, top left.

Different emphases

A stencil design can be given extra subtlety and depth by setting it against a surface with a textured paint finish, such as colourwashing, spattering or woodgraining (see the marquetry-like thistles on the door on the opposite page), or even a perforated screen. Bare plaster walls make an unusual background.

Or, you can give a stencil more interest by applying paint over it, in the form of a pale wash of diluted emulsion or spattered paint, glaze or even varnish.

Paint types and colours

As well as stippling emulsion paint through with a stiff brush (see pp.112–13) you can use eggshell paint or artists' oil paints. With oil-based paints like these it is easier to blend colours for soft shading as the paint stays wet longer. You can also use spray paints to achieve beautiful soft edges by varying the pressure on the nozzle.

Stencils sprayed in gold and silver paint will add lustre to a scheme. The gold colour of the floral design on page 100, top left, added to the glamour of the decor.

STENCIL CARD GUIDES

Card stencils and masks make useful guides for other techniques. Here I used the stencil to draw a pencil guide before applying metal leaf, shown on page 100; on page 81 I used a mask to shield separate applications of paint.

Effects of background
Here it can be seen how different painted backgrounds have different effects on a stencil pattern. One design is sprayed on a grey background, the other is on a red background. Colours can soften or accentuate different parts of the stencil. On the grey background the border is emphasized; on the red background the central part stands out most.

Repeating stencil patterns

*Single images can be repeated to create
an all-over pattern, or to fill a
particular space, as with the thistle
design, below, which was designed to fit
the woodgrained door panels. Repeats
can also be used to create a border
around a room. The early American oak
leaf design, right, overlaps where the
gold colouring of the leaf fades to
nothing. The second stencil, used to add
the black veins on the leaves, is cut with
registration holes to line up the card with
the gold leaves. Traditionally, this
technique of gold colouring is done by
shaking metallic powders on to tacky
goldsize. An easier method is to stipple
on gold paint, as I did here.*

American
oak leaf
stencil

Stencil with
registration
marks, below

Stencilled frieze stippled
with gold paint

Subtle stencil effects

*In complex stencils obvious "bridges" of
card that link the cut out areas together
can be camouflaged for a subtler effect if
the stencil is executed on a perforated
surface, like the wooden screen, below.*

Stencil card and
sprayed stencilling
on a wooden screen,
above

Thistle stencil design (used
with emulsion)

COLOUR VARIATIONS

*A simple stencil constructed from
one piece of card can be partly taped
over or masked so that different
colours can be stippled or sprayed
on separately. In this way colours
can be used to emphasize different
parts of the pattern, and their
qualities balanced to suit the colour
of the background.*

USING PHOTOCOPIES

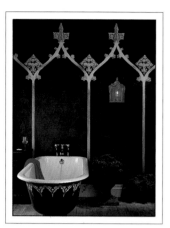

The art of using paper cutouts (découpage) has a historical background of high pedigree. In the late eighteenth century, for example, there was a vogue for découpage *engravings, which were pasted on to walls and coloured. The black and white lines of engravings reproduce well on a photocopier. I take copies from books on historical ornament and use them as an integral part of a room's decoration, either in black and white, as in the bathroom scheme above, or hand-painted. Colour photocopies are also effective (see the French Empire Study on p.56, top left).*

PAPER CAN be glued to any hard surface that has been painted or wallpapered, as well as bare wood, plaster and stiff leather. PVA diluted 1:1 with water is the best all-purpose glue for pasting paper; wallpaper paste is a suitable alternative.

I used diluted emulsion paints for colouring the photocopy shown on the opposite page, but acrylic paints, gouache, artists' watercolours and artists' oil paints can be used instead.

Protecting paper

Paper will discolour and may become damaged if it is not varnished. A coat of diluted PVA is perfectly adequate for protecting cutouts on walls, unless they are likely to get wet, in which case you should use a waterproof varnish, such as EVA or acrylic varnish (see pp.140–41 and pp.152–55). Use a tough oil-based varnish to protect paper glued to surfaces where paper needs to be hardwearing.

To antique your image in the style of Victorian *découpage* apply a coat of amber French enamel varnish and to give it a delicate, cracked appearance apply crackle varnish (see pp.140–41).

Timesaving

There is no need to cut out an intricate design accurately if you are going to paste it to a painted surface because any unwanted areas of photocopy can be painted to match the background colour.

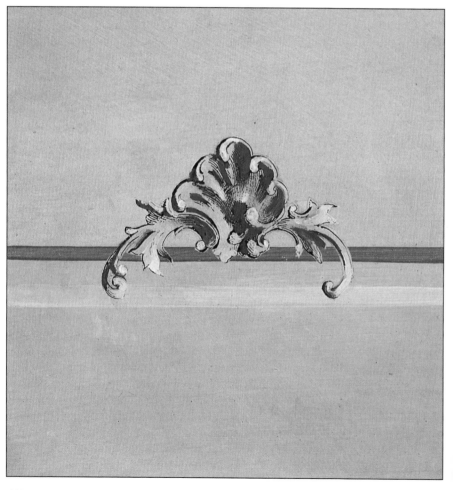

Trompe l'oeil effect, *left. This painted photocopy forms part of the* trompe l'oeil *decoration in the scheme on page 120, top left. It is much quicker to hand-colour photocopies than to paint complex designs from scratch.*

Artists' brush

Long-bristled fitch

Decorating brush

PVA

Scalpel

Craft knife

TOOLS & MATERIALS

Use a scalpel or craft knife to cut out photocopies and a decorating brush to paste and varnish them. PVA is the best all-purpose glue and varnish for paper. For painting, uses a small brush like an artists' paintbrush or fitch.

COLOURED DÉCOUPAGE

I coloured these photocopies of eighteenth-century engravings with artists' watercolours, so they blend in with the tones of the authentic eighteenth-century green of the walls.

1 *Place the photocopy on a smooth, hard surface and carefully cut it out with a craft knife or scalpel while steadying the paper.*

2 *Use a decorating brush to coat both sides of the photocopy with PVA (diluted 1:1 with water). Position it and brush it flat.*

3 *The paper will shrink flat on drying. Paint the photocopy with emulsion (diluted 1:1 with water) the same colour as the background.*

4 *When dry, use an artists' brush to paint the shadows. Use the dark areas of the photocopy as a guide and blend the paint with your finger.*

5 *Paint the highlights with white paint; use the areas of the photocopy that appear to be raised as a guide. Take care to be as neat as possible with the paint.*

6 *Soften the division between the highlights and the background colour by smudging the white paint with your finger. When dry, seal the photocopy with PVA or varnish.*

GRISAILLE

Popular throughout the history of decoration, grisaille *is the simplest and one of the most effective forms of* trompe l'oeil *(visual trickery). Shades of black, white and grey paint are used to imitate three-dimensional subjects, such as stone ornaments and cartouches, and architectural features, like the door frame in the scheme shown, left. In the steps opposite, I demonstrate how to imitate a panel moulding in monochrome on a textured plaster wall; turn to page 120 to see the same moulding painted in colour (a more complex process) and refer to page 120, top left, to see it employed as part of an exuberant and entertaining* trompe l'oeil *scheme for a dining room.*

Pointed fitches

Long-haired lining brushes

Straight edge

Black, white and grey emulsion

FOLLOWING IN the tradition of using water-based paints for *grisaille*, I use water-based emulsion, which is easy to work with and dries fast. Other suitable paints include artists' oil paints diluted with turpentine, which can take up to 24 hours to dry, and home-made gesso paint (see p.156 for how to make this), which dries fairly fast.

Preparation and finishing

Non-absorbent surfaces painted with emulsion are the most suitable for *grisaille*. Surfaces that are already painted with an oil-based paint, such as eggshell, should be rubbed with fuller's earth or whiting (see pp.144–45) to absorb any grease. Protect *grisaille* that is likely to be damaged with a coat of matt oil-based varnish.

Opposite, I show how to imitate a panel moulding, using a logical system of painted lines, which represent light and shadow.

Use a length of moulded dado rail or moulded picture frame as an aid to painting smudge-free straight lines. Place the rail or frame so the ridged edge lies just above the wall. Then, resting the ferrule of your brush on the ridge, paint the line. There is no danger of paint leaking beneath the rail or frame, as it would if you were using a ruler, because the bristles will come into contact only with the wall.

If, after *step 7*, the painted lines look too stark, soften and blend them by lightly brushing over the surface with a decorating brush dampened with water.

Painted picture frame

To imitate a moulded picture frame, use the system of painted light and shadows shown opposite. Redraw the cross-section of a real picture frame four times; indicate the light raised areas and dark recessed areas by each one. Remember to paint mitred corners.

TOOLS & MATERIALS

The most suitable brushes for painting lines are lining brushes and pointed fitches. Use a piece of moulded picture frame (or moulded dado rail) as a straight edge. Dilute the emulsion paints 1:5 with water (except for step 6 *when the dilution should be 1:4).*

The system
Choose a piece of panel moulding to imitate, and sketch it on the wall in cross-section. Hold the moulding flat against the wall and decide on a source of light (I decided on a source above). Use different colours to mark alongside the cross-section where light falls on the raised areas and where shadows occur in the recesses; I used yellow and black here.

1 *In pencil, draw lines that correspond to the areas of light and shade indicated beside the cross-section.*

2 *Apply pale-grey emulsion over the whole area. This will give the moulding body.*

3 *Use a fitch and black emulsion to paint broad lines to represent the lightest shadows.*

4 *To suggest the curve of the moulding, soften the edges of some of the shadows with a damp brush.*

5 *Using a very thin lining brush, paint dark lines to represent the deep recesses and shadows.*

6 *Paint white lines where the moulding would catch the light. Dilute the paint 1:4 with water.*

7 *Paint a "cast" shadow (with raw umber emulsion) over the bottom part of the moulding and the wall.*

TROMPE L'OEIL

*Effects that trick the eye (*trompe l'oeil*) can be used to provide incidental ornament or the subject of a whole wall's decoration, like that shown in the scheme on the left. The techniques I use include using paint and painted photocopies. Unless you are fairly confident in the art of painting perspective, forget the demands of*

landscapes and figures and depict architectural features such as low-relief mouldings and columns, using a system of shadows and highlights (copy from other sources if you like), to make the painted image look three-dimensional.

Paper option *Ready-made paper designs like this are a time-saving alternative to painted* trompe l'oeil. *Blend in the paper by painting it with a diluted version of your wall colour, in this case pale-grey emulsion.*

F OR THE *trompe l'oeil* moulding below I used the *grisaille* technique shown on pages 118–19, replacing the grey background with pale pink and choosing lighter and darker versions of the same colour for highlights and shadows. As with *grisaille* choose an unrelated colour (blue in this instance) for the "cast" shadow. Similarly, for other features, start with an all-over background colour and build up highlights and shadows.

The most useful reference for architectural *trompe l'oeil* is prints of artists such as Piranesi and Leonardo da Vinci. These clearly show areas of light and shade. Look first

at the background colour and note how this and other colours are built up. Observe also the two types of shadow: modelling shadows, which describe the shape of an object, and cast shadows, the shadows it casts.

The traditional media used are distemper and gesso paint (see p.156) but you may find it easier to work with artists' oil paints mixed with a little turpentine or transparent oil glaze, or emulsion.

Colour moulding *This is a colour version of the panel moulding depicted using the monochrome version of* trompe l'oeil, *known as* grisaille, *which is shown on pages 118–19.*

I smudged pencil shading to make a three-dimensional-looking frame for the painted ivy-leaf frieze above. The graphic image below, which I scaled up from a poster design, was simple to paint because there was no shading or blending of colours.

TOOLS,
MATERIALS
& DECORATOR'S
REFERENCE

DECORATING BRUSHES

DECORATING brushes are used to apply and manipulate different sorts of paint in a variety of ways, as well as to apply waxes, pastes and powders.

Styles of brush

There are many designs of decorating brush: round, domed, flat-ended, pointed and chiselled, and they range in size from one hair wide to 25cm (10in) wide.

Though the scale of the job and the medium in hand dictate the size and basic composition of the brush needed, many design variations are simply due to manufacturers' whims or a particular country's decorating traditions.

But one thing is certain: for nearly all work nothing betters pig bristle. Lily-bristle brushes, made from white hog-hair, are the best decorating brushes you can buy and are worth the investment. The bristles are soft, flexible and have flags (split ends) that disperse the paint and soften out the brush-marks. For advice on cleaning brushes see pages 134–35.

Old but serviceable
emulsion brush

Flat, oval, or round?

The flatter a brush the less paint it can hold, yet flat brushes are the most widely used in the United States and Britain; oval brushes are the most popular design in the rest of Europe. The round brush, which holds a generous amount of paint, is an old British design; the one shown below, right, is quite small by traditional standards.

An old friend, above.
This 10-year-old brush, still in use even though it has a split ferrule, has a flexibility and character all of its own.

Oval brush

Old medium size
flat brush

Lily-bristle
flat brush

Old-fashioned
round brush

DIFFERENT GRIPS

For brushing out or softening hold the brush, as shown, top, and for wide sweeps, as above.

Short-bristled
sash brush

Lily-bristle
sash brush

Wide sash
brush

Medium size
well-chiselled
emulsion brush

Sash brushes
*These 3–5-cm (1–2-in)
brushes are known as sash
brushes because they were
traditionally used for
painting window frames –
in fact they are useful for all
sorts of small-scale work.*

Large well-chiselled
emulsion brush

Short-bristled
emulsion brush

Lily-bristle
emulsion brush
(stained through use)

Emulsion brushes
*The size, bristle length and flexibility of
emulsion brushes make for efficient
coverage with any type of paint. The
bristle ends of the two large brushes
above have been worn to a chisel edge: a
benefit, for this gives a smoother flow.
The thick, short-bristle brush is another
popular design of emulsion brush; it can
also be used as a cheap stippler. The
largest brush is what I call a "tosher"
and is used for covering huge areas.*

123

FITCHES & LINING BRUSHES

FITCHES and lining brushes are used for small-scale and detailed work. Each subgroup has different characteristics and their use varies accordingly. Some of these brushes are designed specifically for decorative painting and others are artists' brushes.

Fitches are extremely useful for painting furniture and picking out mouldings. They come in a variety of shapes, with either round or square ends. Fitch is the old name of a member of the weasel family, from which hairs were plucked to make this type of brush. Today the best fitches are made from white lily bristles (and are rather similar to artists' hog-hair brushes).

Lining brushes made from hog-hair, ox-hair, polyester and sable are used for delicate freehand painting, lining furniture and marbling. Fitches and lining brushes can be used with both water- and oil-based paints.

Lining brushes (left to right): ox-hair liner, hog-hair liner, polyester liner

Pointed fitches, *left.*
These light, delicately-balanced brushes are used for accurate picking-out work. The black-bristled ones are flexible and hold a lot of paint relative to the width of the line produced. The lily-bristle fitch is stiffer and more controlled, and good for depositing paint deep into mouldings.

Large pointed fitch

Thin pointed fitch

Stiff lily-bristle fitch

Sable artists' brush

Squirrel-hair swordliner

Large swordliner

Lining brushes
These are designed for maintaining a thin flow of paint over a long line. Use those made from sable or polyester for thin washes of paint and hog- and ox-hair ones for thicker paints.

Swordliners and sables
Swordliners come in various sizes. They are used for lining, marbling and detailing and work best with thin paint. A sable artists' brush will suffice if you do not wish to invest in a swordliner.

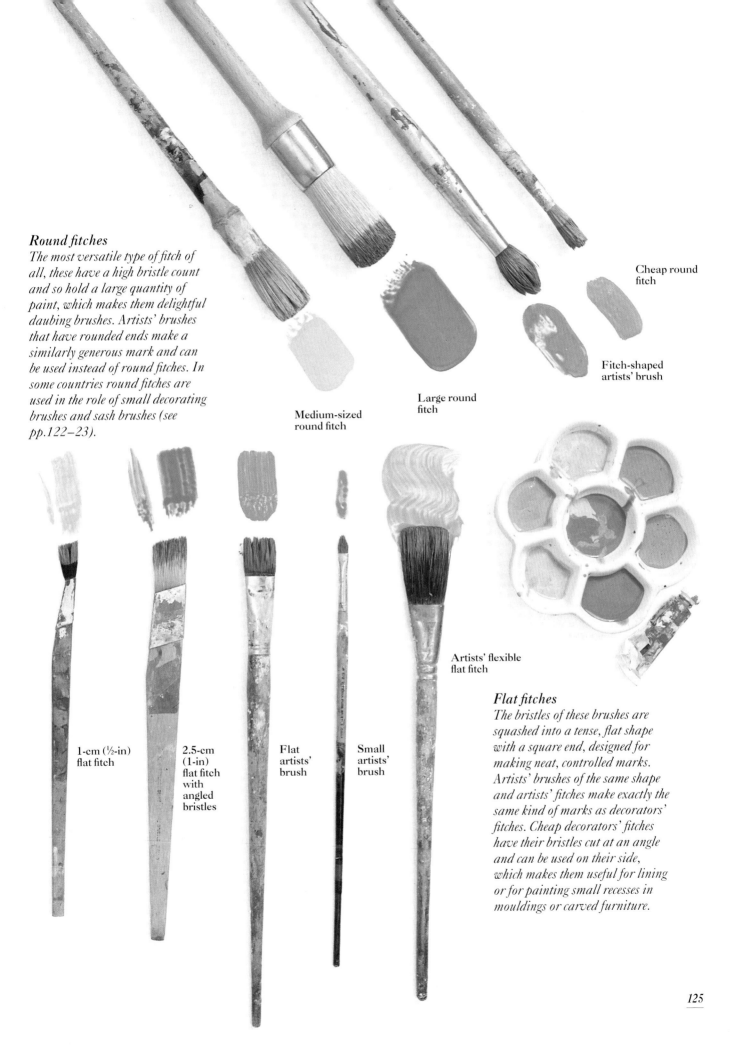

Round fitches

The most versatile type of fitch of all, these have a high bristle count and so hold a large quantity of paint, which makes them delightful daubing brushes. Artists' brushes that have rounded ends make a similarly generous mark and can be used instead of round fitches. In some countries round fitches are used in the role of small decorating brushes and sash brushes (see pp.122–23).

Cheap round
fitch

Fitch-shaped
artists' brush

Large round
fitch

Medium-sized
round fitch

Artists' flexible
flat fitch

1-cm (½-in)
flat fitch

2.5-cm
(1-in)
flat fitch
with
angled
bristles

Flat
artists'
brush

Small
artists'
brush

Flat fitches

The bristles of these brushes are squashed into a tense, flat shape with a square end, designed for making neat, controlled marks. Artists' brushes of the same shape and artists' fitches make exactly the same kind of marks as decorators' fitches. Cheap decorators' fitches have their bristles cut at an angle and can be used on their side, which makes them useful for lining or for painting small recesses in mouldings or carved furniture.

BRUSHES FOR SOFTENING & VARNISHING

S OFTENING brushes are gently pulled over wet paint or glaze to eradicate brush marks and to give a smooth finish. The badger-hair softener is the best and this is reflected in its price; the lily-bristle softener is the next best and is less expensive.

Alternative softener

The dusting brush is an excellent, cheap alternative to badger-hair or lily-bristle softeners. Made from long, soft, hog-hairs set into a resin stock and designed for smoothing wet paint, they also make effective softeners (see p.129 for the other uses of this versatile brush).

It is worth investing in high quality varnishing brushes and treating them with care because with unsuitable brushes you will achieve a disappointing result.

Choosing a varnisher

There are many different types of varnisher, including the chisel-headed brush shown below, which delivers varnish a little at a time, creating a smooth, even layer. Novices sometimes prefer a lighter brush like a long-handled lily-bristle brush or a glider.

As with all brushes, try your hand at as many as you can until you find the one that suits you.

Pointed brush for applying shellac

Brushes for varnishing
Many different types of brush can be used for varnishing, including the chisel-headed lily-bristle brush, which many people use for painting. Gliders are thin, light brushes for applying thin varnishes that need a lot of brushing out. Long-handled brushes with a generous head of bristles, like lily-bristle and hog-hair brushes, are suitable for thicker varnishes that need to flow on to the surface, rather than be brushed out. Varnish brushes should never be used with paint, for minute traces of dried paint will work their way on to your pristine varnished surface. Clean varnish brushes immediately after use and do not store next to paintbrushes.

Small glider

Large glider

Chisel-headed lily-bristle brush

Soft hog-hair brush

Brush for shellac
To apply a coat of shellac (as opposed to shellac varnishing, see p.163) use a pointed brush. Keep the brush solely for this purpose.

Stock and bristles of a decorating brush

Brushes for softening
A dusting brush (also known as a jamb duster) or the stock and bristles of a thick decorating brush can be used as effective softeners for oil glazes and emulsion washes. Make sure that you clean excess paint off the bristles as you work and that no solvent touches the resin stock – it will dissolve.

Small softeners, *right.*
Badger brushes come in a range of shapes, their price varying according to their size. Small badger brushes are designed for softening paints and glazes on accessories and furniture. The fan badger is designed for small areas and mouldings and the pencil badger reaches into corners of frames and the panel mouldings of furniture, pulling out the frequent accumulations of colour that get left there. Other soft brushes such as delicate artists' fans, camel-hair softeners, squirrel mops and even make-up brushes can be used instead of badger-hair brushes.

Dusting brush used as a softener

Badger-hair softener
This brush, which is the crème de la crème *of softening brushes, has entered the mythology of specialist decoration, partly due to its price, which is eight to ten times that of a similar-sized decorating brush. The badger-hair softener is made from the finest badger hairs set into a resin or rubber stock. Only the tips of the bristles are used, to tickle the surface of the paint to a flawless finish. I, like many others, use a dusting brush or lily-bristle softening brush instead. They are cheaper and give a good result.*

Fan badger

Pencil badger

Camel-hair softener

Badger-hair softener

Small artists' fan

Make-up brush

SPECIALIST BRUSHES, ROCKERS & ROLLERS

THE BURGEONING interest in decorative paint techniques, fostered by the Victorians, and the previously unsurpassed displays of graining and marbling at the Great Exhibitions of Paris and London, led to the first-ever organized production of specialist tools.

Until then, the style was for more abstract finishes and artists just made do with the tools they had to hand or made their own.

Though there is now a greater range of specialist tools and brushes on the market than ever before, many just duplicate or approximate the roles of others.

The maximum number of special tools you will ever need for the effects in this book is shown here. Some of these are expensive, but wherever possible I have suggested cheaper brushes that can be used successfully to approximate the marks they make.

Checking roller and oak grain effect

Checking roller
To create an oak grain effect, paint is wiped over the steel plates of a checking roller as it is pushed along a flogged surface.

Stippler and feather
Stipplers are used to lift off flecks of glaze. The large stippler, below left, has long, finely-flagged bristles and leaves a finely freckled impression; a stronger mark can be made by increasing the pressure. If you do not want to invest in a stippler use a lily-bristle decorating brush instead. The feather was dipped in solvent and used to produce the veined lines typical of marble.

Gilding tools, *right.*
The value and fragility of gold leaf means that only the finest camel-hair brushes should be used with it. A gilders' tip is used to handle sheets of gold leaf and a mop (which must be kept grease-free) is used to dust on metallic powders .

Stencilling brushes
These have stiff, tightly-packed bristles and they are used with a brisk, dabbing action.

Camel-hair mop

Large stencilling brush

Stencilling brush made from a fitch

Small stencilling brush

Gilders' tip

Large stippling brush and feather

Lily-bristle
fantail
overgrainer,
right

Synthetic
fantail
overgrainer,
right

Horsehair flogging
brush dragged and
patted into glaze

Dusting brush
used here
for graining

Graining brush
and the mark
it makes

Pencil
over-
grainer

Floggers, dusters and grainers, *above.*

Each of these brushes plays a part in creating realistic woodgrain effects, while the flogger and duster have other uses too. Flogging brushes can be pushed, dragged, patted or even stippled into glaze to produce different wood effects; they also make effective draggers. The ever-useful dusting brush, which makes an excellent cheap softener, mottler and stippler, can be dragged through glaze to make a simple woodgrain impression. Graining brushes make a woodgrain texture that can be softened with an overgrainer or dusting brush. Pencil overgrainers are used to add broad bands of grain.

Rockers and combs

These are used to create authentic-looking wood-grains, fantasy woodgrains and abstract patterns. A rubber rocker will magically create the distinctive heart-grain whorls (shown right) typical of pine, which look especially convincing once the pattern has been flogged, dragged, or softened. It is easy to create fantasy grains and abstract patterns using a comb made of steel or rubber.

Rubber rocker and pine effect

Rubber comb and an
abstract pattern

STENCILS

THOUGH there is an abundance of ready-made stencils available, making your own allows you to be more original and to get the correct scale of design for your purposes. The *fleurs-de-lys* designs here, were inspired by illustrations in a book about medieval ornament, and they are fresh with the spontaneity that mass-produced designs often lack (see the wall in the French kitchen scheme shown on p.112).

Only a few easily-obtainable tools and materials are needed to make and use stencils (the techniques are shown on pp.112–13). I nearly always use oiled manila card rather than acetate. The latter is useful for designs that need to be lined up for repeat runs but slippery to cut and altogether less "user-friendly" than manila card. I use emulsion paint (or sometimes spray paint) for most of my stencilling – they come in many colours and dry fast.

Stencil made from oiled manila card

Freehand designs on tracing paper

Book of medieval ornament

Stencil and mask design
The stencil above has an interesting shape yet its outline is simple enough for the removed cut-out to be used as a mask, shown below.

Design made by spraying paint around a card mask

Transferring designs
A freehand interpretation of a design from a book of medieval ornament, left, is shown on the tracing paper above (on one drawing the area to be cut out has been filled in for clarity). A photocopier with a facility for enlarging and reducing can be used to reproduce and change the scale of a design.

Emulsion paint

Home-made
stencilling brush

Fine artists'
brush

Scalpel and
spare blade

Hand tools
*The time-honoured and cleanest
way to stencil is by stippling with
water-based paints, such as
emulsion. Use a stiff decorating
brush or stencilling brush (make
your own by chopping down the
bristles of an old fitch to a stubble).
Use a scalpel or craft knife to cut
out your stencil and low-tack
masking tape to secure it to the wall.*

Low-tack
masking
tape

Insulating tape
for stencil repairs

Decorative
border made
from photocopies

Using photocopies
*Photocopies can be used decoratively
both in their own right and as an
aid to making stencils. Pasted on to
walls, they are a cheap and easy
way of repeating a motif or making
a decorative border or* trompe
l'oeil. *Once sealed with dilute* PVA,
*photocopies can be colourwashed,
tinted or glazed.*

Outlined stencil
*Outlining a stencilled
shape with a fine artists'
brush or long-haired
lining brush will make
even the simplest design
look like a delicate piece
of handpainting (see
pp.112–13).*

Rubber stamp
*A rubber stamp is an
easy way of repeating an
intricate design and if
used with water-based
paints will last for years.
Most copy shops will
make up a stamp from a
black and white design.*

Rubber stamp

Stippled stencil
with freehand
outlining

Fleur-de-lys
stencil made from
manila card

Stencil card
*Water-based paints curl
the edges of manila card;
coating both sides with
spray paint before using
will prevent this. Store
stencils flat and repair
rips with masking tape
or insulating tape.*

SCRAPERS, SPOONS & OTHER TOOLS

Stiff scrubbing brush

Wire brush

Masking tape

NO DECORATOR should be without a range of "sundry implements": a useful hotchpotch of tools and bits and pieces raided from toolboxes, and, more often than not, from the kitchen, the latter being the reason I so often treat paint mixing instructions as recipes.

Ingenious uses

As you try out new techniques you will discover ingenious new uses for old brushes, tools and other items. A small length of picture moulding, for example, is a useful aid to painting straight lines. The rebate of the moulding serves as a straight edge, raised just above the surface, against which to rest the ferrule of a lining brush and paint a clean, straight line, without fear of it smudging.

Window scrapers take blades and can be used to scrape paint off glass and other surfaces; they have a spacer to allow the necessary margin of paint to be left on the glass when painting window frames.

Another useful little gadget, which I discovered a use for in several techniques, is a little wire mesh basket designed for making herbal tea infusions. It has a handle and opens up so you can fill it with powders, such as powdered charcoal, whiting or fuller's earth, for dusting over surfaces.

Household brushes and tape
Keep a scrubbing brush and a wire brush for cleaning brushes, and masking tape for painting stripes and other shapes.

Wallpaper scraper

Picture moulding

Scrapers
Scrapers are invaluable for mixing filler and small quantities of plaster, making pastes, skimming the dried skin off paint, cleaning surfaces and stripping wallpaper. They range in size from the small black window scraper to the "painters' mate", which has a huge, lightweight blade that can be held as a mask when painting mouldings and straight edges.

"Painters' mate"

Window scraper

Small scraper for mixing pastes

Scraper suitable for cleaning surfaces

Miscellaneous tools

All these tools get used time and time again for mixing and applying paints and solvents. The tea infuser is used for dusting on powders, the screwdriver for opening cans and old kitchen knives for mixing paints, handling small quantities of powders and for fine filling. The kitchen dropper, which has a calibrated side, useful for measuring fluids accurately, can be used for dripping solvents on to painted surfaces. The whisk is used for mixing paints and the ladle and spoon for measuring liquids and powders.

Tea infuser
for powders

Screwdriver

Kitchen
knife

Palette
knife

Kitchen dropper

Kitchen whisk

Spoon

Ladle

Other equipment

Sponges and lint-free cotton rags are used to dab, rag and mottle paint. Natural sponges have a beautiful random quality which you can go some way towards imitating by ripping up a car sponge. For cleaning up, use rags or mutton cloth (also known as stockinette) and, for preparation and finishing, a sanding block and several grades of sandpaper and wire wool, down to flour grade sandpaper and grade 0000 wire wool.

Natural sponge

Scissors

Mutton cloth
and lint-free
cotton rags

Wire wool

Ripped-up
car sponge

Sandpaper and
sanding block

CARE OF BRUSHES

IT PAYS TO take care of your brushes as, treated well, a good brush can last for as long as fifteen or twenty years.

Preparing new brushes

All new brushes, good and bad, have a few loose bristles that should be removed before you use the brush. To do this, tap the ferrule (the metal brace on the brush handle) firmly on a table edge, or spin the brush between the palms of your hands. The loose bristles will then work their way out. (This will also dislodge any dust.)

If this does not work, you can always copy the traditional decorator's trick of breaking in a new brush. This is to use the new brush for exterior painting work, for a while, only bringing it indoors when you are sure no more bristles are going to work loose. By this stage, the shape of the brush tip will have been worked to a tapered chisel head – the standard shape for fine paint-finishing.

Cleaning and storing

Ideally all brushes ought to be cleaned thoroughly on the day they are used, and then dried and stored. It is all too easy to leave a brush standing in a jar of solvent for weeks on end until you find the solvent evaporated away and the brush stiff and bent, its bristles stuck to a cake of grey residue at the bottom of the jar. Yet the point about buying expensive brushes is that you never allow yourself to treat them in such a vindictive way!

Store all brushes in a clean, dry atmosphere, preferably in a cupboard where dust cannot settle on them. And make sure the space is ventilated to stop mildew forming.

If you intend to put away your brushes for more than a few weeks, wrap the bristles in newspaper so the brushes keep their shape, and secure the paper around the brushes with a rubber band.

To store brushes in the long term, drill through the handles of large brushes and suspend them from hooks. Small brushes can be stored upside-down in a jar.

You can leave a brush with paint on for an hour or so, provided that you wrap it in a rag (dampened with water for water-based paints or turpentine for oil-based paints) or tin foil. This will keep out the air and stop the paint drying.

Making a chisel head *Decorators used to bind new round brushes with string, carefully "working in" the bristles to create a chisel head.*

CLEANING BRUSHES

Always start by leaving the brush suspended in solvent (see the table on pp.152–55 for the appropriate solvent) for a few minutes. Work the brush in the solvent until it looks clean, then wash it with warm water and soap. Do not use detergent as it can be too harsh. Rinse the brush well in clean water. It is best not to leave brushes suspended in turpentine overnight, as this tends to harden the bristles. If soaking in water, make sure the water does not cover the handle, which can swell and split. If your brushes have been left standing in solvent for weeks and seem beyond repair, try revitalizing them with a proprietary brush cleaner.

Scrubbing a paintbrush *This is the ideal way of dealing with dried-on emulsion paint.*

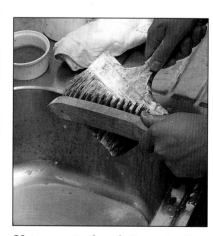

Using a wire brush *For paint that has really dried hard, a wire brush is all you can use!*

Using solvents *Water-based paints such as emulsion are so quick-drying that, no matter how fast you work, they dry on to the brush. To clean, dip the brush into methylated spirits and work the solvent into the bristles with your fingers. Brushes used for oil-based paints such as eggshell should be cleaned with turpentine.*

Using soap *Brushes that have been cleaned with methylated spirits or turpentine should be washed using warm water and simple unperfumed soap. Work the soap well into the bristles so that you reach the ferrule and then wash the brush repeatedly until the rinsing water runs clear.*

Shaping brushes *Flick as much water as possible out of the brush so that it does not take too long to dry. Then comb the damp bristles out using a scrubbing brush. Finally, squeeze the brush between your fingers to shape it.*

Washing large brushes *Another way of cleaning large brushes is to swish them around in a bowl or bucket of water. This lets the water circulate freely between the bristles. The dirty water should be changed frequently.*

BRUSH STORAGE

Decorators have used a variety of gadgets for suspending brushes in water or solvent; modern equivalents are sold today. Hanging up brushes is a traditional method of storage.

Old-fashioned methods *One invention for suspending brushes was a spring system; another used special hooks. A simpler solution was to drive nails into a wooden pail.*

Air ventilation *The best way to store paintbrushes is to hang them up in a ventilated cupboard. This lets the air circulate between them and the brushes will keep their shape much better than if they are stored flat.*

PIGMENTS & HOME-MADE PAINTS

INTERIOR decoration has ancient origins. Over six thousand years ago the citizens of Jericho painted the lower half of their walls with a red pigment, iron oxide, mixed with a binder in the form of a primitive glue. Today's paints, both manufactured and home-made, are not so very different: pigments (concentrated natural or synthetic colours) are mixed with a binder that dries on exposure to the air.

Making your own paint

Home-made paint has pleasant handling qualities and gives a unique finish. The ingredients are cheap and you can make exactly the colour you want.

Pigments are readily available as powder colour and are contained in artists' oil paints for decorating with. Powder colours can be mixed with a range of glues, including PVA and bone glue to make a paste that closely resembles the paint made over six thousand years ago. Artists' oil paints and universal stainers can be mixed with transparent oil glaze to make a translucent glaze suitable for many decorative finishes.

It is important to bear in mind that some pigments have much greater staining power (colour strength when diluted or mixed) than others and some fade in contact with materials. The table on pages 148–51 gives details of their various properties.

Kitchen knife

Palette knife

Tools for mixing
Old kitchen knives and palette knives are ideal for mixing up paints. Use a kitchen sieve to grade powder colours before mixing.

Transparent oil glaze
One of the most useful decorating media is a nineteenth-century invention called transparent oil glaze, which you can buy ready-made or make yourself (see p.156). Pigments, in the form of artists' oil paints, or universal stainers, are mixed with it to create a medium with unique qualities.

Use a spoon for mixing large quantities of glaze and colour

Turpentine or white spirit is used to dilute oil glaze

Artists' oil paint

Transparent oil glaze is opaque in the can and creamy in consistency

Glazes of different strengths are made by varying the ratio of paint to glaze

Rabbit-skin glue can be used to make paint and is an ingredient of gesso (see p.146)

Bone glue (also called pearl glue) is soaked and then heated

PVA can be mixed with powder colours to make paint

Cooled bone glue is a clear jelly

Simple water-based paints

The ingredients above are types of glue, which can be mixed with water and powder colours to make an extremely cheap paint with qualities that are ideal for colourwashing and special effects, such as grisaille *(see pp.118–19). To make a traditional glue-based paint, like that used in the theatre, use an animal gelatin such as bone glue or rabbit-skin glue. These are available from specialist suppliers (see p.164) and need to be diluted with water and heated to transparency in a double boiler (above right) before powder colours are added. Alternatively, you can follow the instructions on page 157 and make paint from powder colours and* PVA, *which is a modern, water-based glue.*

Raw sienna is a tan brown

Burnt sienna, an intense terracotta red, is made from heated raw sienna

Yellow ochre, an intense mustard colour, dilutes to a bright, sunshine yellow

Red ochre is also called red oxide

Earth colours

The earth colour pigments, whether in powder form, like those shown on the left, or contained in tube colours, as artists' oil paints, have the most ancient origins. They are called earth colours because they are dug from the ground and their names often indicate their origin. The Umber colours, for example, come from the Italian region of Umbria, and terra verde *(Italian for "green earth") is exactly that. Their natural charm as colours makes them invaluable for tinting, dulling and antiquing. The earth colour pigments, both in powder and liquid form, are cheaper than other pigments.*

Raw umber is an excellent brown for antiquing (see p.68)

Burnt umber is a richer, more chocolatey colour than raw umber

PROPRIETARY PAINTS

THE ARRAY of paints on the market may at first seem bewildering, but once you know which paint dilutes in which solvent, you can begin to distinguish the main categories of paint. It is the binder in the paint – which is used to hold the paint together – that determines which solvent can be used to dilute the paint and to clean it off brushes. Some paints, such as gloss and eggshell, are oil-based and these are all soluble in white spirit, while others, like emulsion, which are water-based, are water-soluble.

As a general rule, paints that have the same binder can be mixed together. So you can mix emulsion with another water-based paint like artists' acrylic. A look at the information on the side of the paint container will tell you what kind of paint it is and you can refer to the table on pages 152–55, which gives the properties of proprietary paints.

Spray paints
These tough, quick-drying paints (often formulated for retouching car bodywork) are useful for colouring small areas and for stencilling. Different colours can be sprayed one on top of another to give delicate blendings of colour. Look for CFC-free sprays and use in a well-ventilated area.

Water-based inks are available as writing ink, artists' ink or concentrated watercolours

Shading from a spray paint

Spray paints

Gouache and acrylic paint can be mixed with water-based inks

Inks, *above.*
Water-based inks are a useful addition to the painter's repertoire. They can be spattered in antiquing techniques (see p.66) and can be used instead of powder colour for mixing into PVA to make a quick-drying, transparent glaze. Indian ink gives the densest black, even when diluted, and dries to give a waterproof finish.

Primers
Most bare surfaces need a coat of primer so that subsequent coats of paint will bond (see pp.30–43 for surface preparation).

Tube colours
Acrylics and gouache are water-soluble artists' paints. Gouache is denser and has less intense hues than acrylics. Both can be used for colouring water-based paints.

Tubes of water-based gouache

Zinc primer (left) for aluminium

Red oxide primer (far left) for steel

Water-based artists' acrylics

Thick and flexible acrylic primer for canvas

Specialist paints

There are a number of specialist paints on the market, like this paint which creates a broken effect like that of hammered metal.

Hammer-finish enamel paint

Oil-based or alkyd paints

Paints like gloss and eggshell, which are usually loosely described as oil-based, are these days usually bound with a synthetic alkyd resin. They can be tinted with universal stainers or artists' oil paints.

Gloss: an oil-based paint

Household enamel paint

Modellers' enamel paint

Eggshell paint

This oil-based paint gives a reasonably "flat" finish that is the ideal base for oil glazes. It is slow drying and requires even and careful application.

Eggshell: an oil-based paint

Green oil paint mixed into gloss

Paint finishes

Note the different reflective qualities of the various types of paint on the plate, above.

Artists' oil paints

The composition of artists' oil paints – pigment and linseed oil – has barely changed since the fifteenth century. Like universal stainers, they can be used to tint oil-based paints, oil glazes and varnishes.

Paint manufacturer's colour swatch cards

Poster paints

Poster paints are water-based. They are useful for freehand work and for tinting other water-based paints.

Poster paints

Artists' oil paints

Universal stainer – widely available chemical dye

Emulsion paint

This tough, water-based paint can be used to paint walls, floors and furniture. It can be tinted with universal stainers.

Emulsion: a water-soluble paint

139

VARNISHES & GLAZES

VARNISHES are categorized according to their main ingredient and the solvent with which they can be diluted. The three groups of varnish that are shown here are: oil-based (which dilute in turpentine), water-based (which dilute in water), and alcohol-based (which dilute in methylated spirits).

Each type of varnish within these groups has varying qualities and properties and, according to these, different decorative and practical uses (for a summary see the table on pp.152–55).

The conventional role of most household varnishes is to form a protective coating over a plain or painted surface but these, and other types of varnish, can be used decoratively, to create a layer of translucent colour. Some specialist varnishes, such as French enamel varnish, come ready-coloured; most household varnishes do not, but they can be coloured with tube paints or powder colours (see the table on pp.152–55).

Using oil glaze

For a really smooth layer of translucent colour it is best to use transparent oil glaze. It is less sticky than varnish and much easier to manipulate to a flawless finish. It does not dry hard but can be protected with a layer of clear varnish.

Crackle varnish:
a two-part varnish

Crackle varnish

This is sold as a pack of two varnishes that work against each other to create a decorative cracked finish on many surfaces (see pp.66–67). Crackle varnish was invented in eighteenth-century France to imitate the fine web of cracks (known as craquelure*) on Eastern lacquerwork and pottery.*

Tint oil glaze with artists' oil paint or universal stainers

Transparent oil glaze
This versatile medium, which is usually associated with creating faux *finishes, can be used to form a simple, varnish-like tint, its advantage over varnish being that it does not clog the brush, so can be blended into an even layer. It dries soft but can be protected with a hard-drying varnish.*

Transparent oil glaze

Different brands of glaze vary in colour but all dry transparent

Oil-based varnishes
Traditional oil-based varnishes can still be found under names such as "decorative varnish" and "copal varnish". I use these in preference to polyurethane varnishes which, though extremely tough, tend to yellow, and flake when sanded. Goldsize is very quick-drying and is insurpassable for sealing gold paint and metallic powders (see pp.100–101); I also use it as a general-purpose varnish for small areas. Oil-based varnishes can be coloured with universal stainers or artists' oil paints.

Goldsize tinted with artists' oil paint

Polyurethane varnish

Old fashioned oil-based "decorative varnish"

Shellac

Made from a sticky brown goo secreted by the lac insect, shellac is used neat for some techniques (like that on pp.68–69) but when diluted with methylated spirits makes a quick-drying varnish. There are several grades, ranging from standard brown shellac to fine-grade orange shellac. Bleached shellac, sold as white polish, is used for French polishing pale woods.

Standard brown shellac

Amber French enamel varnish

Fine-grade orange shellac (also called button polish)

Red French enamel varnish

White polish is bleached shellac

Sanding sealer

Sanding sealer *Shellac is the main ingredient of sanding sealer, which is used for sealing bare wood prior to varnishing.*

French enamel varnish

Available from specialist suppliers (see p.164), French enamel varnish is made from bleached and chemically dyed shellac. It is manufactured in several colours and is used to stain and varnish wood all in one process. Some colours are bright and coarse, but can be diluted with methylated spirits to create subtler tones. The earthier colours, such as amber and chestnut brown, are amongst the most pleasing.

Water-based varnishes, *right. The past ten years have seen the increased use of acrylic and vinyl resin varnishes that are held in suspension in water. For most general varnishing I use* PVA *and its waterproof sister* EVA *(both vinyl varnishes).* PVA *and* EVA *are cheap, widely available and can be used to seal porous surfaces such as plaster, as a protective varnish for wallpaper and photocopy découpage work (see pp.116–17) and for binding home-made paints (see p.157). For small areas I often use artists' acrylic varnish, which is waterproof and non-yellowing.*

PVA can be tinted with water-based paints

Water-based tube paint

Two types of artists' acrylic varnish, below and right

PVA, like EVA, is white when liquid but dries clear

SOLVENTS

SOLVENTS are most commonly associated with the practical tasks of diluting paints and varnishes and cleaning brushes (see the details on pp.152–55), but they can also be spattered and sponged on to painted and glazed surfaces to make random patterns.

Effects with solvents

The solvents featured here are turpentine (white spirit can be used as an alternative), methylated spirits, water, and acetone. Some paint and solvent combinations have no effect at all, but when there is a reaction it is often dramatic. The results are ideal for marbling (see pp.92–93), scrubbed limewash (pp.52–53) and general patinated effects (pp.104–105). The thinner the layer of paint or glaze on to which the solvent is applied, the more striking the finish will be.

When spattering with solvents, remember always to protect your eyes with a pair of goggles (when spattering with acetone it is important to protect your hands too).

A mottled effect, below, created by turpentine spattered on to wet, transparent oil glaze (tinted with colour)

Turpentine flicked on to wet oil-based paint produces soft patches, left

Turpentine, above, has the same properties as white spirit (also called turpentine substitute)

Turpentine and white spirit
Turpentine is a clear solvent that is distilled from pine tree resin. White spirit (also called turpentine substitute), which is slightly thinner and much more unpleasant smelling than turpentine, is used more widely because it is cheaper. White spirit and turpentine react identically on wet oil-based paints and oil glazes, but do not react at all on dry surfaces. When used on diluted oil-based paints, above, they produce subtle patches, while their effect on oil glaze, left, produces mottled patterns of extraordinary detail. Both are highly toxic.

Acetone
Acetones are a range of complex solvents that react with oil-based paints such as gloss and eggshell. They are dangerous, so should be used with care and never in a confined space. Acetone reacts immediately when spattered or lightly sponged on to wet paint, but must be left for 30 minutes after being applied to dry paint and then rubbed with a clean cloth to reveal a pattern of spot marks and worn areas. Any remaining solvent will evaporate and any untouched areas of softened paint will re-harden.

Acetone flicked on to dry oil-based paint and then rubbed, creates spots and worn areas

Always protect your hands and eyes when using solvents

Methylated spirit can be spattered on to wet or dry French enamel varnish, below

Methylated spirits flicked on to dry emulsion and then rubbed gives a patchy finish, right

The effect of methylated spirits on a layer of wet, diluted emulsion, below

Methylated spirits

Methylated spirits is ethyl alcohol, "denatured" by the addition of naphtha and methyl violet to render it undrinkable. Use it principally to dilute shellac or French enamel varnish (see pp.140–41). You can also flick, sponge or dribble it on to wet or dry emulsion to create a distressed effect. When spattered on to French enamel varnish, left, it creates patterns of a marble-like depth and complexity, similar to those created by turpentine or white spirit on a wet oil glaze; the effect of methylated spirits spattered on to wet emulsion is "flatter".

Methylated spirits

The soft effect of water spattered on to a coat of wet, diluted emulsion

Water

Water is the cheapest of solvents. It is used to dilute water-based paints such as emulsion and can be used to create patterns on surfaces painted with a coat of watered-down emulsion or a wash of PVA. The unique pattern created by water complements that produced by methylated spirits and the two look highly effective when worked together. As with any fluid that is also the diluting agent, take care not to apply too much water, or you will wash the paint away. Water is also used in a number of techniques before applying washes of paint.

Applying solvents

It is easiest to use a brush to flood a horizontal surface with solvent, but for vertical surfaces like walls it is better to use sponges or rags, making sure you wring them out first.

Water is a convenient solvent, but slow to dry

PASTES & POWDERS

Y OU CAN use simple materials to make pastes and mixtures that will transform the most mundane of surfaces, imitating wood, for example, that has the patina of years of dust and polish, weather-worn sandstone, faded terracotta or ancient, encrusted verdigris. *Faux* effects like these have an ancient heritage – in the eighteenth century a mixture of lime, sand and plaster dust was used to imitate stone.

Using plaster

The potential of plaster as a decorative wall finish is often overlooked. Smooth plaster is usually painted, while textured plaster effects tend to be associated with attempts to disguise shoddy structures. Smooth, bare plaster walls have a refreshing elegance – you can colour white plaster by adding powder colours. Ancient plaster walls have a dramatic simplicity that you can imitate by applying plaster over blobs of wax (see the technique on pp.72–73).

Finding suitable materials

Some of the materials shown here, for example whiting and fuller's earth, are only found in specialist suppliers (see pp.164–65) but those like sand and plaster are available from builder's merchants or do-it-yourself shops.

Plastic shapes

Using pastes
Use pastes and powders to transform ordinary plastic shapes, like those above, into pieces of verdigrised ornament or antique wood.

Wet plaster

Textured plaster

Decorators' white plaster

Plaster
Decorators' plaster is available in standard grey or pink, as well as white, which is a useful medium for tinting with powder colours. Like plaster of Paris, decorators' plaster is a gypsum plaster, but because it has a much slower drying time it can be manipulated with a plastic bag or trowel.

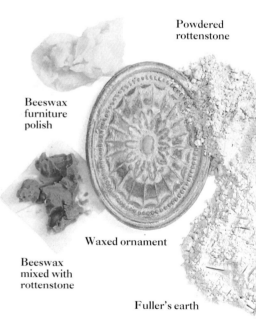

Powdered rottenstone

Beeswax furniture polish

Waxed ornament

Beeswax mixed with rottenstone

Fuller's earth

Gesso
For centuries gesso has been used to prime wood to make a completely smooth finish over which to paint or gild. The basic recipe comprises whiting and rabbit-skin glue (see the instructions on p.156 for how to make this traditional version and a synthetic variation using PVA).

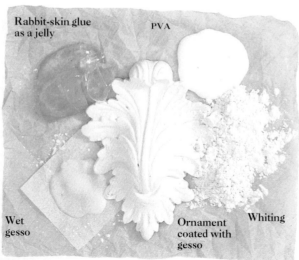

Rabbit-skin glue as a jelly

PVA

Wet gesso

Ornament coated with gesso

Whiting

Waxes, *above.*
Antiquing waxes are easy to make and can be used as a decorative finish in their own right, or in the ageing and distressing of wood, where they are used to simulate the effect of years of dust worn into furniture polish. To make an antiquing wax, mix beeswax polish and a little turpentine and then add colour in the form of fuller's earth, powdered rottenstone or powder colours. Alternatively, oil paints or even shoe polish can also be used to colour wax.

Mixing pastes

Most pastes are extremely quick-drying and mucky, so mix them in disposable containers such as jam jars and yoghurt pots. Use a knife for mixing – a brush will become hopelessly clogged. Keep lids and plastic film at hand to cover the containers and prevent the pastes drying up too quickly.

Palette knife and rottenstone

Emulsion

Whiting

Whiting can be patted on to the damp paste

Methylated spirits

Paste for imitation verdigris

Verdigris paste

Some metal effects, such as the imitation of verdigris, require a crumbling texture. Use a paste made from emulsion paint, whiting and methylated spirits. The whiting adds body to the paste and the methylated spirits curdles the paint to give it a crumbly consistency.

Beeswax furniture polish

Limed ornament

White powder colour

Liming wax

Liming wax

Wood used to be disinfected with a paste of caustic lime. Now an inert antiquing wax is used. This contains beeswax furniture polish and a harmless white pigment such as white oil paint or powder. It is simple to make but is available ready-made. Liming wax can also be used for antiquing plasterwork.

PVA

Sand

Sand and PVA paste

Sand texture

A sand texture is used for imitating rust and some types of stone, where an all-over gritty texture is needed. Cover the surface in glue (either spray glue or undiluted PVA) and pat, blow or throw dry sand at the surface. Use fine grade sand for small objects such as lamps.

Sand

PVA

Deep sandstone texture

To imitate the highly-textured relief of some of the more distressed and eroded types of stone, apply a paste on top of the sand texture, shown left. Mix sand and undiluted PVA to make an extremely thick paste and apply this with a spatula. Paint the surface when the paste is dry.

GILDING MATERIALS

THE ART of gilding has a mystique about it – justifiably so in the case of water gilding, which is a highly specialized skill, but oil gilding (see pp.100–101) is simple and it need not be expensive.

Oil gilding involves laying transfer leaf (either real gold or its inexpensive counterpart, Dutch metal) over a layer of a tacky varnish called goldsize. For a silky smooth finish, the area to be gilded is prepared with several layers of gesso. This comes ready-made in white, red or ochre or you can make your own using the ingredients shown below (see p.156 for detailed instructions). Red gesso glows through transfer leaf and any tiny cracks in it to give a rich warmth and antique appearance; yellow ochre gesso serves to disguise cracks in the transfer leaf and intensify its colour.

Powders

Metallic powders (available in a wide range of colours, including gold) can be shaken on to tacky goldsize for a gilt finish. They can also be mixed with varnish to make gold paint and used with transfer leaf to imitate an effect called combination gilding; the real version is created by a combination of oil and water gilding. Suppliers of gilding materials are listed on page 164.

Oil-gilded emblem patinated with French enamel varnish

Self-adhesive gold tape

Rabbit-skin glue as a powder, below, and as a jelly, after heating, below left

Ready-made gesso comes in red, ochre and white

Sprayed surface gilded with transfer leaf

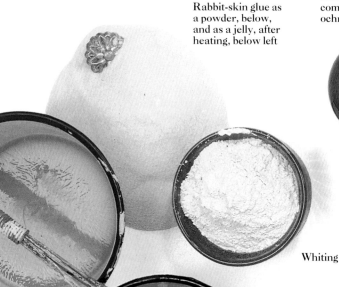

Whiting

Home-made gesso mix

Gesso

Layers of gesso are painted on and polished to make a surface smooth before gilding (see pp.100–101). Gesso is available ready-made or you can make your own from whiting (powdered chalk) and rabbit-skin glue or PVA (see p.156 for gesso recipes).

Special effects

Water gilding is often done over a layer of coloured clay (usually red), which shows through cracks in the gold leaf. You can imitate this effect with oil gilding, by applying transfer leaf over coloured gesso (buy this ready-made or colour home-made gesso with red ochre powder colour) or red spray paint. Use self-adhesive gold tape to imitate strips of gold leaf, and French enamel varnish, dilute emulsion or ink to patinate your work (see pp.104–105).

A sheet of transfer gold leaf, below, on a sheet of transfer Dutch metal leaf, with some loose leaf, below left

Metallic powders, *below. These fine, dusty powders are available from art shops and come in a wide range of colours. They can be mixed with* PVA *or varnish to make an effective paint and shaken on to tacky goldsize with a brush or tea infuser to make a flawless gilt finish. In combination with oil gilding using transfer leaf, metallic powders can be used to imitate an effect known as combination gilding, which is traditionally created by a complicated technique involving water gilding and oil gilding.*

Ornament gilded with transfer leaf and powder

Gold powder

Metal leaf
Transfer gold leaf and its cheap, effective alternative, transfer Dutch metal leaf, come on a waxed paper backing. Loose leaf is mostly used for water gilding.

Ornament gilded with gold powder

Goldsize, left and in its container, is an adhesive varnish

Oil goldsize
This varnish is used as the adhesive for metal leaf and metallic powders. It is sold as oil goldsize or Japan goldsize (the latter dries faster).

Gold powder can be shaken on to tacky goldsize using a brush

147

PIGMENTS & COLOURS

MANY OF THE paints that I use are ready-coloured paints, such as emulsion and eggshell. Some techniques, however, call for home-made paints coloured with pigments (concentrated natural or synthetic colours), which are available as powder colours, or are present in tube colours, such as artists' oil paints, artists' acrylics and gouache, each of which has a different binder. These can also be used to alter the colour of different types of ready-coloured paint, and to tint varnishes. Artists' oil paints and universal stainers can be added to transparent oil glaze to colour it.

Colour characteristics

On the right and overleaf is a selection of colours, shown in the form of artists' oil paints. Identical colours, with the same names, can also be obtained as artists' acrylics, gouache, powder colours and universal stainers.

The characteristics of different pigments vary enormously. Some are opaque, others almost transparent; some have good covering power, others very little. Whiting, for example, is translucent when mixed with oil-bound media, but opaque in water. *See overleaf for a key to the table headings.*

Matching colours

Alongside the artists' oil paints are a paint manufacturer's swatches, which show just how closely many of the tube colours can be matched with proprietary paints. Because of this I frequently refer to proprietary paints like emulsion by the names of the pigments they match. However, a proprietary paint does not have the same properties as the tube colour or the powder colour it matches.

	QUALITIES/USES
CRIMSON LAKE	Originally made from cochineal, lake colours are now manufactured chemically. See also scarlet lake. Lake colours are intense and brilliant but they tend to fade in light.
ROSE MADDER	A soft, translucent red. Originally produced from the madder plant, this pigment is now manufactured synthetically. Mixes with white to give beautiful pinks.
SCARLET LAKE	A similar pigment to crimson lake (above): an intense pigment suitable for all decorating purposes.
CADMIUM ORANGE	Cadmium-based pigments, though toxic, have good covering power, are intense and stable over long periods of time. Also available in red, which can be used as an alternative to scarlet lake.
CHROME YELLOW	One of a range of powerful, intense colours derived from chromates of lead.
CADMIUM YELLOW	See also cadmium orange (above). Good covering power; intense, stable colour.
YELLOW OCHRE	One of the earth colours: a beautiful, warm, brownish-yellow used under gilding. Heated yellow ochre produces purply red ochre.
RAW SIENNA	An ancient, brownish-yellow earth colour from Italy, useful for toning down colours, antiquing and mixing with raw umber.
BURNT SIENNA	An earth colour, produced by heating raw sienna. A good terracotta-brown, producing delightful pinks when used in washes.

Table continued overleaf

STAINING POWER	OPACITY	ALKALI RESISTANCE	LIGHT PERMANENCE	COMPOSITION	TOXICITY
****	☐☐☐	✗	(2 bulbs)	Dyes precipitated on to alumina.	skin 2, inhalation 2, swallowing 2
***	☐☐	✗	(4 bulbs)	Madder plant extracts; chemical dyes.	skin 1, inhalation 1, swallowing 1
****	☐☐☐	✗	(2 bulbs)	Dyes precipitated on to alumina.	skin 2, inhalation 2, swallowing 2
***	☐☐☐☐	✗	(3 bulbs)	Cadmium sulphide, cadmium selenide.	skin 1, inhalation 5, swallowing 5
*****	☐☐☐☐	✗	(3 bulbs)	Lead chromate.	skin 4, inhalation 5, swallowing 5
***	☐☐☐☐	✗	(3 bulbs)	Cadmium sulphide.	skin 1, inhalation 5, swallowing 5
****	☐☐☐☐☐	✓	(4 bulbs)	Iron oxide.	skin 1, inhalation 1, swallowing 1
***	☐☐☐	✓	(4 bulbs)	Clay containing iron oxides and aluminium oxides.	skin 1, inhalation 1, swallowing 1
***	☐☐☐	✓	(4 bulbs)	Clay with iron oxides.	skin 1, inhalation 1, swallowing 1

Symbols

This table makes use of a system of pictorial symbols for grading the various properties of pigments.

Low staining power, for example, is marked ∗; good staining power ∗∗∗∗∗ and so on.

Similarly, the toxicity level of the pigments increases from 1 to 5 (extremely toxic) in the following three categories:

(hand)	skin contact
(bottle)	inhalation
(ladle)	swallowing

Pigments with 5 skin contact symbols should be handled wearing gloves. Alkali-resistant colours are marked with a tick, non-alkali-resistant colours, with a cross.

Powder colours

When using powder colours exercise particular caution because in this form the pigments can be very dangerous. Always wear gloves (pigments can be absorbed through the skin and accumulate beneath fingernails), and a paper dust mask, which is essential to avoid inhaling small particles of dust. Pigments that have five inhalation symbols should *never* be used in powder form.

KEY TO TABLE HEADINGS

Qualities/uses
Characteristics of the pigment and its applications.

Staining power
The pigment's ability to penetrate a surface and stain it. If the staining power is high you will need a comparatively small quantity of pigment relative to a given area.

Opacity
Opacity is a good indication of covering power. Yellow ochre, for example, is opaque and covers most background colours in one coat, while others, like rose madder, dry to a translucent finish, making them suitable for tinting transparent oil glaze. The opacity of whiting varies according to whether it is bound in oil or water.

Alkali resistance
Lime is an alkaline compound capable of bleaching colours. To tint plaster that contains lime, or gypsum plaster, use powder colours that are alkali resistant.

Light permanence
Some pigments fade on exposure to natural light; their permanence is indicated here. Manufacturers of artists' oil paints also have a rating system given on the side of the container.

Composition
The chemical formulation of the pigment, excluding its particular oil or water binder.

Toxicity
Many pigments are highly toxic; some are even carcinogens. Never swallow or inhale pigments and do not allow highly toxic ones to touch the skin, specially powder colours. Store all pigments out of the reach of children. Read the chemical formulation of all the pigments you use, and take particular care if they have a five-symbol toxicity rating or are in the "highly toxic" list on the opposite page.

	QUALITIES/USES
BURNT UMBER	A rich, chocolatey-brown earth colour, which is manufactured by heating raw umber pigment.
RAW UMBER	A slightly green/grey-brown earth colour. An extremely useful neutral pigment, good for toning down other colours.
TERRA VERDE	An Italian earth colour, "green earth" is a pleasant green with a bluish-grey tinge.
CHROME OXIDE	A soft pigment, with a pleasant organic shade of green. Extremely opaque. Good mixing qualities, and so frequently used in water- and oil-bound paints.
PERMANENT GREEN	This versatile green (also known as guignet's green) is resistant to acid, alkali and light, but is only moderately enduring when applied in a thin wash. As it does not discolour it is good for solid colour.
ULTRAMARINE BLUE	Meaning from "across the sea", this ancient, beautiful, deep blue pigment was originally very costly as it was made from lapis lazuli.
COBALT BLUE	An ancient pigment, valued for its brilliance and purity of tone. Ideal for solid work and flat areas of detail. Works well in oil glazes, as it has a good degree of translucency.
ZINC WHITE	Also known as Chinese white. Used in some undercoats. Excellent covering power. Has a hardening effect when used in oil glaze.
TITANIUM WHITE	Effective, very white pigment. Used in liming pastes. Slightly chalky, and so is usually hardened with zinc oxide.
WHITING	Ingredient of distemper, whitewash and gesso. Good opacity in water; poor opacity in oil-bound media and wax.

STAINING POWER	OPACITY	ALKALI RESISTANCE	LIGHT PERMANENCE	COMPOSITION	TOXICITY
***	□□	✔	3 bulbs	Clay containing iron and manganese silicates and oxides.	1 hand, 4 bottles, 4 watering cans
***	□□	✔	4 bulbs	Clay with iron and manganese silicates and oxides.	1 hand, 4 bottles, 4 watering cans
**	□□	✔	4 bulbs	Natural silicates of iron and magnesium.	1 hand, 1 bottle, 1 watering can
***	□□□□□	✔	3 bulbs	Chromic oxide.	3 hands, 4 bottles, 4 watering cans
****	□□	✔	3 bulbs	Viridian (an oxide of chromium), mixed with zinc chromate and barites.	4 hands, 4 bottles, 5 watering cans
*	□	✔	4 bulbs	Sodium silicate, plus aluminium and sulphur.	1 hand, 1 bottle, 1 watering can
***	□□□ (in water) □ (in oil)	✔	4 bulbs	Cobalt oxide, aluminium oxide.	1 hand, 2 bottles, 1 watering can
	□□□□	✔	4 bulbs	Zinc oxide.	1 hand, 2 bottles, 2 watering cans
	□□□□□	✔	3 bulbs	Titanium oxide.	1 hand, 1 bottle, 1 watering can
	□□□ (in water) □ (in oil)	✔	4 bulbs	Chalk (calcium carbonate), ground washed and dried.	1 hand, 1 bottle, 1 watering can

Other highly toxic pigments: handle with extreme caution; (avoid in powder form)
Antimony pigments
Lead-based pigments
Chrome-based pigments
Cadmium-based pigments
Phthalo-based pigments
Barium yellow
Cobalt yellow
Emerald green
Carbon black
Lemon yellow
Naples yellow
Scheele's green
Strontium yellow
Vermilion

Other toxic pigments: handle with care
Alizarin crimson
Alumina
Cerulean blue
Cobalt green
Cobalt violet
English red
Indian red
Ivory black
Mars black, brown, red, orange, violet, yellow
Prussian blue, Paris blue
Terra rosa
Ultramarine blue, green, red, violet

Paints, Varnishes & Solvents

This table shows the composition, properties and uses of the various types of paint and varnish used for the techniques demonstrated in this book.

Solvents

Paints and varnishes can be diluted with particular solvents, which are also used for cleaning brushes. See the column headed "Solvents" in the table for further information. In addition, some solvents can be used in association with various paints and varnishes for decorative effects (see pp.142–43).

Toxicity

Great care is needed when handling paints and varnishes. While some of their ingredients are poisonous, the solvents used in conjunction with them are, for the most part, highly toxic, the obvious exception being water. Such solvents as well as paints and varnishes can be absorbed into the body in three ways, denoted in the table by three symbols, used on a scale from 1 (mildly toxic) to 5 (highly toxic).

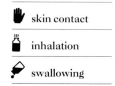

skin contact

inhalation

swallowing

The poisonous effects of solvents depend on how they enter the body.

Safety precautions

When using paints, varnishes and solvents, work in well-ventilated areas. Label containers carefully, and keep them out of the reach of children. Never eat, drink or smoke when working. When using some substances it is also advisable to wear gloves and goggles. A respiratory mask protects against the inhalation of fumes and a dust mask against powder colour particles.

TYPE	USES	MIX WITH
EMULSION PAINT (matt and vinyl silk)	Water-based paints for general interior decorating: ceilings, walls and wood. May be diluted for colourwashing or thickened with whiting for textural effects. Vinyl silk has a greater degree of sheen.	Water (for diluting), universal stainers, powder colours, water-based tube colours e.g. gouache and artists' acrylics.
EGGSHELL, GLOSS PAINT & OIL-BASED UNDERCOAT	Oil-based paints for general interior painting. Can be diluted for hard-wearing washes. Eggshell is the perfect basecoat for oil glaze. Oil-based undercoats can be tinted for a very matt finish.	Univeral stainers, artists' oil paints, transparent oil glaze.
GESSO, DISTEMPER & BUTTERMILK (casein) PAINTS	Traditional water-based paints, which all have similar properties, for walls and furniture. Now less fashionable but gesso is still widely used to prepare surfaces, for relief work and as a ground for gilding.	Gouache, powder colours.
LIMEWASH	Traditional paint used on the exterior of buildings. Was also used on interior walls to give a distinctive, chalky, matt finish, instead of white distemper.	Alkali-resistant powder colours.
SPRAY PAINTS	Convenient way of applying paint for some techniques, such as stencilling, basecoats for gilding, and imitation verdigris.	Nothing.
PVA & EVA	PVA is a good binder for home-made paints (made with powder colours) that are used for colourwashing. It is useful for sticking down and protecting paper from dirt. EVA is similar but waterproof.	Emulsion paint, universal stainers, powder colours, gouache, artists' acrylics, water-based inks.
ARTISTS' OIL PAINTS	These are the paints used in oil paintings. Excellent for colouring transparent oil glaze, varnish and eggshell paint. Mix with beeswax furniture polish and turpentine to make good antiquing colours.	Transparent oil glaze, eggshell paint, gloss paint, beeswax furniture polish and oil- and resin-based varnishes that are soluble in turpentine.
POWDER COLOURS	Use to make home-made paints for colourwashing and freehand detail. Also useful for tinting proprietary paints, varnishes and plaster.	Water, emulsion, PVA, transparent oil glaze, oil-based and polyurethane varnishes.

Table continued overleaf

ADVANTAGES	DISADVANTAGES	SOLVENTS	COMPOSITION	TOXICITY
Inexpensive. Relatively clean. Quick-drying (1–3 hours). Can be tinted to the shade you require. Water-proof finish. Enormous range of colours.	Dark colours lack depth and richness. Finish may need protection as dirt cannot be easily washed off.	Water. When dry can be softened and removed with methylated spirits.	Pigment, synthetic resins and PVA (or polyacrylic binder suspended in water).	(hand; bottle; 2 brushes)
Hard, durable finish with good depth of colour. Enormous range of colours.	Eggshell and gloss need an undercoat and, on an absorbent surface, an initial coat of primer. Slow-drying (6–12 hours). Unpleasant fumes, which are dangerous in quantity.	Turpentine and white spirit.	Pigment, synthetic drying oils and synthetic alkyd resin. Traditional drying oils (such as linseed) and natural resins have been superseded by synthetic compounds.	(hand; 3 bottles; 4 brushes)
Soft texture and chalky colours. Gesso and casein may be highly polished, giving great character to a finished surface. Allow the passage of moisture.	May deteriorate in the container. Poor covering power. Adhere only to porous surfaces. Not waterproof. Soft and liable to rub off when wetted (except casein). Not widely available.	Water.	Pigment (often chalk) in water, natural binder, such as animal gelatin or casein (a by-product of cheesemaking) and, in some cases, a water-proofing oil.	(hand; bottle; brush) *
Disinfectant and insecticidal properties. Good for old walls, which need to "breathe", because it allows the passage of moisture.	Highly caustic when wet. Only semi-waterproof when dry. Rubs off easily.	Water.	Water, slaked lime (calcium hydroxide) and a water-proofing agent, such as tallow.	(4 hands; 4 bottles; 4 brushes)
Quick-drying to a hard and perfectly smooth finish. Adhere to most surfaces. Fast to apply. Can be reactivated when dry with solvent.	Highly toxic substances with an unpleasant smell. Spray "fallout" can be considerable, coating all surfaces in the immediate vicinity. Often contain hazardous propellants: avoid these.	Xylene, acetone and toluene.	Pigment, nitro-cellulose lacquer (or acrylic lacquer in petroleum distillate) and propellant.	(2 hands; 4 bottles; 4 brushes)
Versatile media with excellent sealing and binding properties. Quick-drying. Cheap and widely available.	Often dries slightly glossy and remains soft. PVA is not waterproof.	Water.	PVA: polyvinyl acetate dispersed in water. EVA: ethylene vinyl acetate.	(hand; bottle; brush)
Intense, concentrated colours that tolerate much dilution. Good for mixing with other oil-based media. Slow-drying therefore workable. Wide range of colours.	Degree of translucency and covering power variable. Some colours are expensive, which makes it prohibitive to use them over large areas.	Turpentine, white spirit.	Finely ground pigment, linseed oil and drying oils.	(hand – 3 hands; bottle – 4 bottles; brush – 4 brushes) *
Powder colour washes have a particularly pleasing quality. Can be mixed together dry for accurate colour matching. Cheap and widely available.	The properties of different powder colours vary enormously. Generally need protection to prevent colour rubbing away. Many are extremely toxic.	Water.	Finely ground pigment (naturally occurring or chemically manufactured).	(hand – 3 hands; bottle – 4 bottles; brush – 4 brushes) *

* Toxicity varies according to colour. See pages 148–51.

COMMONLY USED SOLVENTS

Protection is advised when using any of the solvents below in large quantities. People with sensitive skin or allergies are sometimes affected by turpentine and white spirit even when used in small quantities.

Methylated Spirits
Contains: methanol, wood alcohol, denatured alcohol, methyl violet. Inflammable.

✋ *Can lead to unconsciousness and organ damage. Wear gloves.*

🗢 *Can lead to unconsciousness and organ damage. Wear mask.*

🖌 *Fatal; can cause blindness.*

Turpentine
Contains: pure turpentine, gum spirits, gum turpentine. Inflammable.

✋ *Causes skin allergies. Wear gloves.*

🗢 *Irritant vapours. Wear mask.*

🖌 *Fatal.*

White Spirit (turpentine substitute)
Contains: petroleum distillates. Cheaper than turpentine, and has the same properties. Inflammable.

✋ *Wear gloves.*

🗢 *Irritant vapours. Wear mask.*

🖌 *Fatal.*

Acetone
Contains: acetone (one of the ketone compounds). Highly inflammable.

✋ *Irritant. Wear gloves.*

🗢 *Can cause unconsciousness.*

🖌 *Causes nausea and abdominal pain.*

TYPE	USES	MIX WITH
GOUACHE/ARTISTS' ACRYLICS	Concentrated tube colours in a water-soluble base used for solid colour work and washes. Gouache traditionally used on gesso for decorating furniture.	Water, emulsion, PVA.
UNIVERSAL STAINERS	Versatile, intense colours, in a liquid form, that can be combined with virtually all types of oil- and water-based paints and glazes to produce a wide range of colours.	Water, emulsion, eggshell, transparent oil glaze, oil-based varnish and polyurethane varnishes, woodstain.
TRANSPARENT OIL GLAZE	Used with artists' oil paints or universal stainers to make a coloured glaze, which can be used for woodgraining, dragging, antiquing and stippling.	Artists' oil paints, oil-based (alkyd) paints, universal stainers, oil-based varnish and polyurethane varnish (for a glossier finish).
SHELLAC & FRENCH ENAMEL VARNISH	Shellac is used as a sealing varnish, for antiquing, and to coat stencil card; French enamel varnish is used to stain glass.	Shellac products can be mixed with each other and readily accept woodstains soluble in methylated spirits.
SANDING SEALER & KNOTTING	Sanding sealer is used to seal wood before painting and varnishing to prevent discoloration. Knotting seals knots in resinous wood.	Other shellac-based products and methylated spirits.
GOLDSIZE	Used as an adhesive base for applying gold leaf and metal powders. Available as oil-based and water-based goldsize.	*Oil:* oil-based paints, artists' oil paints, powder colours, transparent oil glaze. *Water-based:* pigments or gouache.
GENERAL-PURPOSE OIL-BASED VARNISHES	Traditional varnishes, such as copal varnish and decorative varnish, for protecting all manner of paint finishes. Now superseded by widely available polyurethane varnishes.	Oil-based paints, artists' oil paints, powder colours, universal stainers, transparent oil glaze.
POLYURETHANE VARNISH	All-purpose varnish, which is hard and durable, for coating many interior surfaces. Available in matt, semi-gloss and gloss finishes.	Oil-based paints, artists' oil paints, powder colours, transparent oil glaze.
ACRYLIC VARNISH	Excellent, new generation of quick-drying water- or petroleum distillate-based varnishes. Suitable for all types of decorative varnishing.	Water-based version mixes with universal stainers and powder colours.
BEESWAX FURNITURE POLISH	Used to polish paintwork or furniture. Can be coloured for use as antiquing wax or liming wax.	Artists' oil paints, powder colours, powdered rottenstone, fuller's earth, shoe polish.

ADVANTAGES	DISADVANTAGES	SOLVENTS	COMPOSITION	TOXICITY
Strong colours with excellent staining powers. Tolerate dilution to make vividly coloured washes. Artists' acrylics are waterproof when dry.	Expensive. Artists' acrylics dry very rapidly (1 hour). Gouache does not dry waterproof.	Water.	Concentrated pigments in a water-soluble base.	(gloves 1–4) * (bottles 2–4) (brushes 1–4)
Colours are very strong and so can be diluted. Good mixing qualities. Inexpensive and adaptable.	Limited range of colours available. For colour variation mix with ready-coloured paints, such as emulsion and eggshell.	Turpentine, white spirit.	Dyes bound in a solvent base.	(gloves 2) (bottles 3) (brushes 4)
Cheap and effective way to extend colour. Dries in 6 hours. Good workability for up to half an hour.	Tends to form skin in tin. Yellows significantly if exposed to sunlight. Protect with a coat of varnish as it dries soft.	Turpentine, white spirit.	Whiting (chalk), linseed oil (or a synthetic alkyd resin), drying oils and white spirit.	(gloves 2) (bottles 2) (brushes 4)
All shellac products are quick-drying. Shellac: several grades available including standard brown, fine-grade orange shellac (button polish) and bleached shellac (also called white polish).	All brittle and yellow (except for white polish). Need to work quickly as they dry rapidly but can be dissolved in alcohol.	Methylated spirits.	Flake shellac (crystals of resinous substance secreted by the lac insect) and alcohol. French enamel varnish is shellac-based and is available in several colours containing aniline dyes.	(gloves 3) (bottles 3) (brushes 3)
Quick-drying; provide effective barrier on wood.	Brittle; knotting is dark-coloured, so unsuitable for use under pale washes (use white polish instead).	Methylated spirits.	Flake shellac (see "Shellac", above) and alcohol.	(gloves 3) (bottles 3) (brushes 4)
Oil: quick-drying, hard, glossy varnish with excellent flow properties. *Water-based:* very user friendly.	*Oil:* slightly brittle. Liable to form skin and partially oxidize in can. Does not dry to as hard a finish as polyurethane varnish. *Water-based:* soft when dry.	*Oil:* turpentine, white spirit. *Water-based:* water.	*Oil:* traditionally made of linseed oil, resin and drying oils. Often a blend of natural oils and resins. *Water-based:* water-type glue suspended in an acrylic medium.	(gloves 2) (bottles 3) (brushes 4)
Extremely high-quality finishes. Can be sanded.	Often slow drying times, due to the low resin content. Sometimes brittle.	Turpentine, white spirit.	Natural oils and resins, with drying oils.	(gloves 2) (bottles 3) (brushes 4)
Cheap, widely available and easy to use. Dries in 4–6 hours to produce a hardwearing, strong finish.	Sometimes yellowish and brittle. Liable to flake when sanded down.	Turpentine, white spirit.	Synthetic resins and oils.	(gloves 2) (bottles 3) (brushes 4)
Water-based version is quick-drying, tough and very clear. Pleasant to work with.	Petroleum distillate-based version is highly toxic. Use water-based where possible. Toxicity rating here is for water-based version only.	Varies according to composition.	Tough acrylic resins dispersed either in water or petroleum distillate solvent (xylene or toluene).	(gloves 1) (bottles 1) (brushes 1)
Flexible and versatile. Easily removed with solvent. Waterproof. Polishes well. Pleasant to work with.	Needs regular applications to maintain finish as it is soft. If overheated, emits toxic fumes and degrades.	Turpentine, white spirit.	Soft beeswax and other waxes, such as hard carnauba wax or synthetic silicone wax in solvent (usually turpentine substitute).	(gloves 1) ** (bottles 5) (brushes 5)

*   Toxicity varies according to colour.
**   Toxicity risk from inhalation only if overheated.

RECIPES

THE FOLLOWING recipes are for making your own decorating materials. In some cases the recipes I have included are for products not readily available from decorators' suppliers or DIY stores; in other cases they are for techniques that use a preparation that is not available commercially. See also page 159 for calculating the quantities of paint, varnish or glaze you will need.

STENCIL CARD/OILED PAPER

If you are unable to obtain stencil card (oiled manila card) make your own following this recipe.

What you need

| Thick cartridge paper or manila card |
| Linseed oil or shellac or knotting |

Brush both sides of the paper or card with linseed oil and leave it to dry for a week. The oil makes it pliable, which is important if you intend to stencil a curved surface. Alternatively, brush the card with shellac or knotting, to soften and seal it. These techniques can also be used to strengthen decorative papers to make lampshades or screens.

TRANSPARENT OIL GLAZE

This is used in many techniques. If you have difficulty obtaining it, follow this recipe. When dry, protect the glaze with a coat of matt varnish.

What you need

| 0.5 litres (1 pint) turpentine |
| 0.3 litres (12 fluid ounces) ready-boiled linseed oil |
| 0.2 litres (8 fluid ounces) dryers |
| 1 tablespoon whiting |

Mix the ingredients together using a balloon whisk. Store the glaze in an airtight jar or can.

LIQUID GUM ARABIC (CRACKLE MEDIUM)

A commercial crackle medium can be used for a cracked paint effect, but gum arabic is an excellent substitute.

You can buy this from artists' suppliers as gum water, ready dissolved, or as crystals, which can be dissolved in boiling water to a single cream consistency at the ratio of 0.5 kilogram (1 pound) crystals to 1–1.5 litres (2–3 pints) water.

CRACKLE VARNISH

Crackle varnish is used to produce a delicate, cracked finish called craquelure; see pages 66–67. You can buy it ready-made or make your own. Both have two parts: an oil-based varnish and a water-based varnish. For the first varnish use goldsize, and for the second, liquid gum arabic, the crackle medium described above, adding a drop of washing-up liquid to prevent it from splitting open.

FRENCH ENAMEL VARNISH

To 0.5 litre (1 pint) of white polish add 1 eggcup of alcohol-soluble woodstain to the required intensity.

TRADITIONAL GESSO

Gesso (see p.144), is applied in layers to create a smooth surface on which to gild. Rabbit-skin gesso is applied warm. It cools quickly to a firm jelly, allowing a rapid build-up of layers. When using warm gesso, remove the skin which forms and add a little water.

What you need

| $\frac{1}{3}$ cup rabbit-skin glue powder |
| 0.35 litres (14 fluid ounces) boiling water |
| 0.25 kilograms (8 ounces) whiting |

Place the glue powder in a *bain-marie* (double boiler). Slowly pour on the boiling water, stirring until all the granules are dissolved (to make glue). Sift in whiting ($\frac{1}{3}$–$\frac{1}{2}$ of the total volume) until you have a thick paint.

If you buy the glue as coarse granules, soak them overnight in 0.35 litres of cold water. They will swell into a jelly; heat this in a *bain-marie*.

Gesso can be coloured with powder colours; traditional gesso colours are red and yellow ochre.

MODERN GESSO

Modern PVA gesso has all the qualities of rabbit-skin gesso, but dries more slowly. I use this in preference to commercial acrylic gesso, which is difficult to scrape and polish.

What you need

| $\frac{1}{3}$ cup PVA |
| $\frac{1}{3}$ cup water |
| Whiting |

Dilute the PVA 1:1 with water and mix thoroughly. Sift in whiting ($\frac{1}{3}$–$\frac{1}{2}$ total volume) until you have a thick paint.

GESSO PAINT

This can be used instead of emulsion in grisaille work, see pages 118–19. Make the paint by adding powder colour to gesso. Follow the recipe for traditional gesso, but instead of whiting, add a 1:3 mixture of whiting and powder colour. When dry, the gesso can be polished with wire wool and beeswax polish.

DISTEMPER

This ancient paint, which is still available commercially, allows the passage of moisture, so is useful for painting the walls of old houses where dampness may occur. Here is a simple home-made version.

What you need

| 10 kilograms (20 pounds) whiting |
| 4.5 litres (1 gallon) water |
| Powder colour (or universal stainers) |
| Hot rabbit-skin glue (see Traditional Gesso) or PVA |

Sift the whiting into the water until a peak appears above the surface. Leave to soak overnight. The following day discard the top 5 centimetres (2 inches) of clear water. Add 5–10% of glue by volume. Tint with powder colour or universal stainers mixed with water.

LIMING WAX

Liming wax is used to lime open-grain woods (see pp.58–59) and to antique plaster (see pp.70–71). It is widely available ready-made, but is inexpensive and easy to make.

What you need

| 1 tin beeswax furniture polish |
| Titanium white powder colour |

Heat the beeswax polish gently in a *bain-marie* (double boiler) until liquid. Add ⅓ of its volume of titanium white powder colour and stir. Pour into a pot, and allow to set.

SAFETY NOTE Always heat the wax gently. If over-heated, it produces highly toxic fumes.

LIMING PASTE

Use liming paste instead of liming wax when the surface you wish to lime needs to be varnished. Wipe off any residue on the surface with a damp cloth.

What you need

| 1 tablespoon titanium white powder colour |
| 0.5 litres (1 pint) water |
| Hot rabbit-skin glue (see Traditional Gesso) or gum water (see Liquid Gum Arabic) |

Mix the titanium white powder colour with water to the consistency of single cream. For every pint of this mixture, add 6–7 tablespoons of rabbit-skin glue (heated in a *bain-marie*: see Traditional Gesso) or 3–4 tablespoons of gum water.

MAKING WASHES

There are various ways of preparing washes (thin paints) for use in colourwashing techniques and for painting a thin wash of colour over a different coloured basecoat. The following recipes are the three you need for the techniques used in this book. (See also pp.46–51).

Emulsion wash

This is a very versatile wash and one that I use most frequently.

What you need

| Emulsion paint |
| Water |

Put the full-strength paint you wish to dilute in a bucket. Add a little water, stirring to remove lumps.

Dilute 1 part paint with between 1 and 10 parts water for colourwashing. Note the proportions you use. This is important when working on a large project as emulsion washes separate out and need to be mixed to the same strength on a daily basis.

Water-based wash

This wash can be reworked with a damp sponge or brush when dry, but needs to be protected with an oil-based varnish because it can be rubbed off.

What you need

| Powder colour |
| Water |

Mix the colour with a little water to a creamy consistency. As a rough guide, 3 tablespoons of powder colour mixed with 1 litre of water will be sufficient for colourwashing a room. Stir the paint continuously as you work.

PVA wash

For painting small areas you may wish to use writing ink, artists' acrylics or gouache instead of powder colours, but these are expensive to use on large areas.

What you need

| Powder colour |
| PVA or rabbit-skin glue (see Traditional Gesso) |
| Water |

Mix the colour with a little water to a creamy consistency. Add 5–10% glue by volume as a binder. (If you use hot rabbit-skin glue, mix the colour with hot water so that the glue does not cool rapidly to jelly).

Dilute this mixture to the consistency you need: add approximately 8 parts water for colourwashing or for half tones in *grisaille* and *trompe l'oeil* work.

The thinner the paint, the more quickly the powder colour will settle to the bottom. You will need to stir it back into the paint continually as you work.

TINTING MEDIA

A useful decorating practice is to tint various media with colour. The following recipes explain how.

Tinting emulsion

Use powder colours, artists' acrylics, gouache or universal stainers.

What you need

| Powder colour, artists' acrylic, gouache or universal stainers |
| Water |
| Emulsion paint |

Mix the colour with a little water first. If using universal stainers, mix with a little emulsion first, and ensure that you do not add more than 1 tablespoon of stainer to 5 tablespoons of emulsion, or the paint may not dry properly. Add this mixture to the emulsion, stirring thoroughly to mix the colour evenly.

Tinting transparent oil glaze

When choosing a colour to tint oil glaze, bear in mind that the glaze will begin to yellow slightly three to four months after it has been applied. Red, for example, will become more orange and pale blue will turn green. For this reason, try to avoid tinting glaze with light colours, or choose a water-based paint instead of glaze. A way of impeding the yellow cast of glaze or varnish is to add a drop or two of white eggshell paint to the glaze when colouring them. The quantities given below may vary depending on the staining power of the colour (see the table on pp.148–51).

What you need

| Approx 7–10 centimetres (3–4 inches) artists' oil paints squeezed from the tube |
| Turpentine |
| 0.5 litre (1 pint) oil glaze |

Squeeze the paint into a container. Add a small amount of turpentine to thin it out, and stir well with a brush to make a smooth mixture. Add the glaze, mixing carefully to distribute the colour evenly. Tiny dots of undissolved colour turn into garish streaks when brushed out.

Tinting varnish/eggshell/gloss

Follow the method for tinting transparent oil glaze, above, substituting the oil glaze with varnish (polyurethane or oil-based), eggshell or gloss paint.

Tinting plaster

White plaster powder can be mixed dry with powder colours before it is applied to walls. Some pigments are not alkali-resistant, and the lime content of plaster will cause them to fade completely within a couple of months. Choose only alkali-resistant pigments (see the table on pp.148–51). For a pleasant parchment colour mix approximately ½–1 cup of raw sienna powder colour into a bucket of white plaster. Then, following the manufacturer's instructions, mix the coloured plaster powder with water.

HINTS & TIPS

SOME OF the materials in this book may be familiar to you, others may not. Here is some general advice on how to buy and store materials, and some special tips on varnishing paint finishes.

Protecting paint finishes

Varnish can be used to protect any decorative paint finish but it is particularly useful for glazework and water-based washes, which become damaged easily. Take into account the role the surface has to perform as well as the sort of paint you are protecting when selecting a varnish (the table that appears on pp.152–55 gives a handy summary of the uses and properties of different types of varnish).

General purpose oil-based varnishes and polyurethane varnish are the toughest wearing and most waterproof. They are suitable for protecting paint finishes in bathrooms, kitchens and areas likely to be subject to scuffing from children and animals.

Transparent oil glazes will only accept oil-based varnishes but water-based paints such as emulsion, or home-made washes can be protected with oil- or water-based varnishes, including diluted PVA (this is protective but not waterproof) and acrylic varnish.

BUYING & STORING MATERIALS

Buying in bulk is usually cheapest and most products have a shelf-life of many months, if not years, if correctly stored. Some materials have special storage requirements but as a general rule keep them in dry conditions away from light or extremes of temperature. Avoid keeping materials anywhere freezing temperatures may occur, such as in a shed. Below are some special tips.

Gelatin-based glue
Gelatin-based glues such as rabbit-skin glue and bone glue are available in quantities ranging from ½-kilo (1-pound) to 5-kilo (10-pound) bags. They have an unlimited shelf-life providing they are kept in their powder or granule form and away from damp or insects. Once mixed with water they begin to rot after only a few days. For this reason make up only the quantity you need at any given time.

Gold leaf and metallic powders
The cost of real gold leaf varies according to the carat of the gold. Pure 22-carat gold will never tarnish but Dutch metal (this is not real gold) will dull, even in the book it comes in, over a number of years. Once Dutch metal has been applied, protect it with varnish to prevent oxidation and subsequent dulling of the finish. Metallic powders are available in containers ranging from small jars to ½-kilo (1-pound) bags. They

should be varnished to prevent the finish becoming dull. See the entry for powder colours for storage tips.

Paint and varnish
Replace the lids of paint and varnish tins firmly and providing that the lid seal is not damaged, store the tins upside-down. This ensures that any skin effectively forms at the bottom of the container. Before re-using paints, remove the skin and then stir or shake thoroughly. Do not shake any type of varnish as this introduces air bubbles, which show when the varnish is brushed out. Keep some brushes specifically for varnishing as varnish can loosen dried paint in brushes, spoiling the finish.

Plaster
It is important to keep plaster dry, but no matter how careful you are, it has a limited shelf-life of only a few months, after which it begins to absorb moisture and go gritty, which makes it unusable. Plaster's drying time increases after only several weeks of storage.

Powder colours (including whiting)
Small quantities are sold in jars, larger quantities of about ½ kilo (1 pound) upwards usually come in bags. Keep powder colours and metallic powders in airtight jars with screw-top lids and store them in a dry place. Because they are toxic and should never be inhaled, always

spoon them out carefully (never pour them) and avoid jars with flip-top lids, which tend to jerk the powder around on opening.

Shellac
This is available in bottles ranging from 250 millilitres (½ pint) to 5 litres (1¼ gallons). Shellac has a shelf-life of about a year. As shellac contains methylated spirits, which evaporates at low temperatures, it tends to thicken over several hours of exposure to air. It can be thinned with methylated spirits.

Stencils
Stencils are best stored flat, each layer covered with paper to prevent the patterns from catching each other and ripping.

Transparent oil glaze
This is sold in tins in the same quantity as paint: ½ litre (1 pint) upwards. Different brands look a slightly different colour in the container but this will not affect the colour when used. Glaze has a shelf-life of about a year or so.

Waxes
Waxes and wax polishes sometimes harden in the tin, even if never opened. You can revitalize them by placing the tin in a *bain-marie* (double boiler) and heating it very gently until the wax is soft; then mix in a little fresh turpentine.

Obtaining perfect results

To give varnished paintwork a perfect, smooth finish apply several coats of varnish, lightly sanding with 220 grit paper between coats.

When the last coat is thoroughly dry, use 0000 grade wire wool, dipped in beeswax furniture polish, and buff the surface as though you were polishing a piece of furniture. This will remove any small imperfections and pieces of grit in the surface and give a beautifully silky and reflective surface, free of pits, bumps and all the little particles of dust and grit that usually seem to settle on varnish as it dries. Ten minutes later buff with a duster. This method of finishing is particularly useful for special effects where the material imitated is shiny, for example marble.

Redecorating surfaces

Standard manufactured paints, like gloss and emulsion, can be sanded or washed down as appropriate and repainted. With varnished finishes you can either key the surface with sandpaper or use a proprietary stripper to remove the varnish completely. Wax finishes such as liming and antiquing can, with patience, be removed and redecorated with paint. Rub the surface with turpentine, followed by detergent and water, and then sand to provide a key for the paint.

Transparent oil glaze can be sanded down and painted with an oil-based undercoat prior to being redecorated with oil- or water-based paint or glaze. This is hard work and time consuming, so is only suitable for furniture or small areas, like dados. (You should not expect to achieve a perfectly smooth finish.) If you are planning to glaze whole walls, consider putting up lining paper. This can simply be stripped off prior to redecorating.

Green decorating

Virtually every area of decorating touches on one or another environmental issue. There are pros and cons for both animal-based products and chemically produced ones. Though some people object to using products with animal glues in, for example, the argument for them is that they are biodegradable. Synthetic glues, like PVA, on the other hand, are not animal-based but they do contain chemicals that do not biodegrade.

Not all aerosol paints contain CFCs but many release other harmful solvents into the air. Look out for and try to buy only those that are labelled CFC-free on the container and are indicated as being environmentally friendly.

Some types of brush are made from animal bristles. Badger-hair brushes are made from badger bristle imported from China and the Far East. Badgers are a protected species in many countries. For softening glazework, I use a lily-bristle softener instead of a badger-hair softener. Only in softening watercolour work does a badger-hair softener give a superior finish to any other brush.

Paint and solvent disposal

Many paints and solvents do not break down in the water treatment system so it is important not to dispose of solvents (except for methylated spirits or water) and paints containing solvents down the drain. Instead, pour them into old, empty paint containers, carefully marking the outside with the type of solvent or paint.

Never mix different types of solvent and avoid using old food containers as not only may the contents be mistaken but some solvents may dissolve the container – with disastrous results. Always secure the lids of the containers tightly and keep out of the reach of children.

Check with your local authority to see if they offer facilities for the disposal of waste products such as these. If they do not, the liquid wastes will have to go out with the rest of the household rubbish and either be burned or buried at the local municipal dump.

QUANTITIES

It is impossible to be exact because coverage will depend on how liberally you apply the material, the absorbency of the surface being decorated and the weather (if it is warm paint evaporates and you need to apply more). The quantities in the table below will give you an idea of how much paint or varnish you would need for one coat on the walls of an average size room with a floor area of 4.5 × 4.5 metres and a height of 3 metres (15 × 15 × 10 feet). This gives a wall area of 60 square metres (67 square yards). The amount of wash you need depends on how thin you make it.

Paint type	Number of litres	Number of gallons
Primers	7½	1½
Undercoat	7½	1½
Emulsion	7½	1½
Varnish	5	1
Eggshell	7½	1½
Gloss	7½	1½
Glaze	2	½
Wash	1–2	¼–½
Distemper	7½	1½

Pastes and powders are used in special finishes for tiny decorative objects, furniture and panelling.

ANTIQUING WAX For an average size chest of drawers: a 500-gram (1-pound 1-ounce) tin of beeswax furniture polish, about 250 grams (8 ounces) of powder to mix with the wax (either powder colour, fuller's earth or rottenstone).

LIMING WAX For an average size chest of drawers: one 500-gram (1-pound 1-ounce) tin of beeswax furniture polish and not more than 500 grams (1 pound 1 ounce) of titanium white powder colour.

METALLIC POWDER 100 grams (3½ ounces) is enough to gild an average lamp base.

A LIST OF TERMS & NAMES

Adam, Robert (1728–92) Scottish architect and designer, a leading figure in the neo-Classical movement in British domestic architecture.

ageing variety of abrasive techniques for simulating the effect of time and wear on new paint, wood, plastic, or plasterwork.

aniline dye synthetic pigment found in some paints and varnishes.

anthemion honeysuckle or lotus flower motif or fan-shaped leaf design.

Anthemion in lily-leaf frame

antiquing decorative process that imparts painted surfaces with a false sense of age, so mimicking the discolouration caused by dust and dirt.

arabesque surface decoration, originally found on Arabic paintings, consisting of intertwining leaf, flower or animal forms, or rhythmic designs.

architrave moulded frame that surrounds a doorway, arch, window or wall panel.

armillary sphere a model of the celestial sphere.

armoire large cupboard, usually decorated and with two doors.

Art Deco design style of the inter-war years (named after the 1925 *Exposition des Arts Décoratifs* in Paris) that was heavily influenced by Cubist art and contemporary mechanical forms.

Art Nouveau late nineteenth-century style of art and architecture, opposed to the Classicism of the immediate past.

Arts and Crafts movement late Victorian group of artists who advocated a revival of traditional craftmanship and pre-industrial values.

Aztec characteristic of the art and culture of the Aztecs, an ancient Mexican Indian civilization.

bain-marie double boiler designed for heating substances slowly in cookery and useful for making gesso.

Bakelite the first entirely synthetic industrial plastic, patented in 1907.

Baroque rich European style of architecture and decoration, popular during the seventeenth and eighteenth centuries, chiefly characterized by its floral lines, confidence, theatrical use of ornamentation and grandeur.

bas-relief sculpture that projects slightly from the background but is not detached from it.

Bauhaus design school based in Germany during the 1920s that sought to dismantle the barriers that separate decorative art and engineering.

beading moulding originally designed to resemble a string of beads and used for edging and ornamentation.

Biedermeier style of interior decoration and design that is a version of early nineteenth-century Classical revival styles, such as Empire. The name is that of a German fictional character.

Boucher, François (1703–70) French Rococo artist and designer whose work is typical of eighteenth-century French courtly art.

Brescia city in Lombardy, Italy, known for the red-brown marble that is quarried locally.

brocade heavy, opulent silk with raised patterns, originally worked in gold or silver thread.

butter muslin unbleached muslin, cream in colour.

Byzantine art style that flourished during the sixth century, and, later, from the ninth to the eleventh century, in Byzantium (later Constantinople), and which combined elements from ancient Greece, Oriental culture and Christianity.

cabriole S-shaped design of furniture leg, widely used on early eighteenth-century chairs.

cachepot literally "pot-hider". An ornamental container used to house flowerpots.

calico plain, coarse woven cotton originally from India.

Carrara town in Tuscany, renowned for its white, grey-veined marble.

cartouche panel bearing inscriptions or emblems, often in *trompe l'oeil*.

caryatid sculptured female figure or bust, usually used to support a ceiling, or the architrave, cornice and frieze above a door or fireplace.

castellation resemblance to a castle wall created by the inclusion of battlement- and turret-like patterns.

censer vessel in which incense is burnt over charcoal during ecclesiastical ceremonies.

Cézanne, Paul (1839–1906) leading French post-impressionist painter whose work is characterized by the careful placing of textured brushstrokes in rich tones of colour.

CFC abbreviated form of chlorofluorocarbon, an environment-threatening substance used in the manufacture of some aerosol sprays.

cheesecloth loosely woven cotton fabric, originally used to cover cheese.

chevron regular zigzag line, often used in medieval heraldic designs.

Chinoiserie term for Chinese pieces of decorative art of the seventeenth- and eighteenth-century Western style that coupled contemporary European forms with Oriental motifs.

chintz closely woven, medium-weight cotton fabric, usually glazed and traditionally printed with a colourful floral design on a light background.

chisel head shape of the bristles of a decorating brush which have worn down obliquely at the side with use, thus improving their performance.

clair bois literally, "pale wood". A technique used to imitate the polished finishes of light-coloured woods.

Classical architectural or decorative stylistic motifs prevalent in the designs of Greek or Roman antiquity.

Cliff, Clarice (1899–1972) English pottery designer, associated with the Art Deco movement.

colourwashing simple water-based paint technique used to produce a softly textured, patchy finish, achieved by applying several layers of thin paint.

combination gilding method of gilding where two or more techniques are used together to give the impression that the finer technique alone has been used.

combing technique in which the teeth of a decorator's comb are scraped through a surface glaze.

Castellation

complementary colours any pair of colours that, when placed on a colour wheel, occupy opposing positions. The complementary of any primary colour (red, yellow, blue) is the secondary colour made by mixing the other two.

composition paste of rosin, glue and whiting used for producing mouldings.

Cooper, Susie (b.1902) British ceramicist of the Twenties and Thirties.

corbel projecting architectural bracket, often of stone or brick, that supports a cornice or beam.

cornice external feature projecting from the upper wall, or a moulding used to conceal the joint between the top of a wall and the ceiling.

crackleglaze see *craquelure*.

craquelure decorative glaze finish developed in eighteenth-century France to reproduce the fine network of cracks on Eastern lacquerwork and pottery. Also known as *crackleglaze*.

creamware earthenware that possesses a deep cream colour.

dado lower part of a wall, between the dado rail and the floor.

dado rail projected horizontal moulding traditionally running at waist-height along a wall, dividing the dado from the upper wall.

damask silk or linen fabric, with a lavish textural pattern.

découpage method of decorating walls and objects with paper cutouts.

Delftware tin-glazed earthenware from the Netherlands, traditionally in a blue and white colour combination.

Della Robbia fifteenth-century Renaissance Florentine family of sculptors who used a glazed ceramic medium for decorative sculpture, usually depicting a religious subject framed by a floral wreath.

dentil ornamental moulding; one of a repeat of rectangular, evenly spaced blocks, usually placed underneath a Classical cornice.

distemper group of paints formed by mixing pigments with water, bound with casein, glue or egg, which were widely used before the introduction of emulsion paints.

distressing process of artificially abrading a new surface to create the appearance of old age.

dragging technique of pulling a long-haired brush through wet transparent oil glaze, or distemper, to produce a series of fine lines on walls or furniture.

dry-brushing paint technique that keeps the bristle surface of a brush relatively dry in order to build up a cloudy effect, or to touch with paint the highlights of a textured surface.

dryers chemicals added to decorating materials to speed up their drying rate.

earth colours oxide pigments, such as raw umber, that are made from refined clays and minerals dug from the ground. Available as powders or liquids, they have a natural, timeless quality that makes them ideal for tinting, dulling and antiquing.

ebonized treated with colour to look like ebony.

egg-and-dart pattern, often found on carved architectural mouldings, comprising a row of oval shapes interspersed with arrows.

Empire grandiose French style, that mixed Classical decorative devices with Egyptian and Napoleonic imagery.

Cornice with egg-and-dart moulding, top, and dentils, below

faience European decorated style of tin-glazed earthenware.

faux effects literally, "false" effects. Finishes created to imitate another material, such as marble (*faux marbre*) or wood (*faux bois*).

ferrule metal brace on a paintbrush, used to strengthen the handle and grip the bristles.

filigree delicate ornamentation or tracery, often produced with fine wires of gold or silver.

finial terminal part of any ornamental projection, in the form of a spire or vase, for example, that crowns buildings or furniture.

flagged bristles pig bristles that are naturally split at the end. Brushes with "flags" give a superior finish.

flat finish matt, non-greasy finish.

fleur-de-lys old French motif that takes the form of a stylized lily or iris flower.

fly-spotting finish created by spattering paint, coloured glaze, varnish or ink on to a surface to convey a feeling of age.

fossilstone marble marble in which fossilized animal and plant forms create a mottled pattern.

French polishing treatment of a wooden surface with French polish to give a highly reflective, smooth finish.

fresco durable painting, usually found on walls and ceilings, created by incorporating watercolours directly into wet plaster surfaces; the technique was perfected in Renaissance Italy.

frieze broad horizontal band on the upper part of a wall that is decorated separately from the rest of the room with stencils, paintings, wallpaper or plasterwork.

gilding method of colouring surfaces gold, either by the application of gold leaf or gold paint.

Gill, Eric (1882–1940) English sculptor, engraver and typographer.

gingham checked or striped textile, usually woven from two differently coloured yarns.

Gothic architectural style, of twelfth-century French origin, widely adopted throughout Western Europe until displaced by the Classical influences of the Renaissance.

Gothic arch pointed arch, characteristic of medieval Gothic architecture.

Gothic Revival robust Gothic style of the mid-nineteenth century, noted for its sombre authenticity and display of medieval pomp.

Gothick early- to mid-eighteenth-century decorative style that celebrated the more exuberant elements of the medieval Gothic style, interpreting them in a contemporary setting.

gouache opaque water-based paint, in which the pigments are bound with glue or gum arabic.

grisaille visual trick that harnesses monochrome shades of paint to represent areas of light and shade and thus create, on a flat surface, the illusion of a three-dimensional ornament or an architectural feature.

Gropius, Walter (1883–1969) German architect and designer, Director of the Bauhaus school, from 1919 to 1928.

gypsum plaster standard plaster for interior walls, for patching surfaces and for producing mouldings.

half tone any colour tint judged to be halfway in tone between a given hue and white.

hemp scrim open-weave fabric made from the hemp plant.

hessian plain, coarse fabric, woven from rough fibre and used to make upholstery canvas.

icon Byzantine type of oil painting, with a prescribed set of religious images executed on a wooden panel.

inlay form of decoration on flat surfaces, such as furniture, made with a pattern of holes filled with materials, such as coloured woods, metals or mother-of-pearl.

Kandinsky, Wassily (1866–1944) Russian-born expressionist painter who pioneered a purely abstract style of art. He taught at the Bauhaus until it was closed.

kelim flat-woven tapestry rug, manufactured in the Middle East, typified by the use of brilliant colours and bold patterns.

Klee, Paul (1879–1940) Swiss painter and etcher whose work harmonized formal and imaginative elements.

lacquerwork Oriental decoration that is lacquered in order to provide a strong, high-gloss surface.

Lalique, René (1860–1945) French designer and craftsman, renowned for his Art Nouveau glass pieces.

Landseer, Sir Edwin Henry (1802–73) English realist painter, famous for his studies of animals in landscapes.

Langley, Batty (1697–1751) architect, furniture designer and author, partly responsible for the revival of interest in ogive arches and rosettes that marked the Gothick style.

lapis lazuli blue mineral, used both as a gem stone and as the pigment known as ultramarine blue.

limewash substance composed of slaked lime and water that is used for whitening exterior walls. Also known as whitewash.

liming decorative technique that harnesses liming wax to leave a white pigment in the grain of bare wood, creating a mellow finish.

lincrusta patented nineteenth-century type of cast plastic.

linenfold panelling a style of panel, which is moulded or carved in a design intended to mimic the pattern created by folded cloth.

Lloyd Loom furniture machine-made, closely-woven furniture (especially chairs), patented by the American, Marshall Lloyd.

low relief see *bas-relief*.

Mackintosh, Charles Rennie (1868–1928) Scottish artist, architect and furniture designer, allied to the Art Nouveau movement.

majolica style of earthenware with a thick, white glaze coloured with pigments.

marbling variety of paint techniques designed to recreate artificially the appearance of marble.

marquetry decorative veneer composed of inlaid shapes of exotic woods, bone, metal or ivory.

mask cut-out card shape used to cover a surface and so provide a barrier against a layer of paint.

matchboarding form of cladding in which long wooden boards are held together with tongue-and-groove joints.

Mayan characteristic of the art and architecture of the so-called ancient American Indian civilization.

memento mori (Latin) "remember that you must die": object that serves as a reminder of human mortality.

milk paint primer paint, at one time applied to furniture, based on a protein found in milk.

mitre joint right-angle corner formed when two strips of material, especially wood, each with an edge sloping at a 45⊕ angle, are joined together.

Modernism a style which developed in the fine and applied arts in the early part of the twentieth century, based on a rejection of traditional approaches in favour of more industrial, unornamented genres.

Moorish associated with the art, architecture and culture of the Moors, who established dominance in North Africa and in southern Spain in the eighth century.

Morris, William (1834–96) major English designer, painter, poet and exponent of the decorative arts. A leading figure in the Arts and Crafts movement, he was also an important influence on the Pre-Raphaelites.

mosaic decorative design produced from the assembly of small pieces of stone, marble or glass.

muslin fine, woven cotton fabric used for curtains, hangings, etc.

mutton cloth variable-weave cotton cloth (also known as stockinette).

neo-Classical relating to the eighteenth-century European movement, inspired by the architectural forms of Classicism and characterized by a sense of proportion and harmony.

New Bauhaus design school formed in Chicago following the close of the Bauhaus by the Nazis in 1933.

obelisk square or rectangular stone monument, tapering to a pyramidal point at the top.

Odeon wall lamp Art Deco shell-shaped glass lamp, once installed in Odeon cinemas in Britain.

ogee decorative S-shaped moulding.

ogive arch characteristic Gothic arch, with ogee-shaped sides; popular in eighteenth-century Gothick design.

onyx ornamental marbled stone.

Orientalist a member of a Victorian movement of designers and artists, typified by an interest in Oriental design and motifs.

ormolu ornament of cast-metal alloy, that is gilded industrially.

Moulding with ogee section

panel moulding moulding consisting of small, plain surfaces, that are either inlaid or raised.

papier-mâché layers of paper, or paper pulp, mixed with paste, which dry to form a light but tough material.

parquetry type of inlay of flooring where wooden tiles are laid to form geometrical patterns.

patina colour and texture that appears on the surface of a material as a result of age or atmospheric corrosion.

pelmet structure used to conceal the top edge of a curtain or blind.

pickled another word for woods that have been limed.

picture rail moulding running along the top of a wall to take the hooks from which framed pictures hang.

pietra serena type of stone widely used in Florentine Renaissance architecture.

pilaster shallow, rectangular section of a pillar, added to the face of a wall for ornamental interest.

Piranesi, Giovanni Battista (1720–78) Italian designer, engraver and architect whose major works include the series of etchings named *Le antichitá Romane*.

porphyry purplish rock embedded with crystals of feldspar, which can be simulated with spattered paint.

portico interior and exterior canopy supported on columns or brackets above a doorway or entrance.

post-impressionist term referring to certain artists operating after the Impressionist movement of art in nineteenth-century France.

Pre-Raphaelite brotherhood association of mid-nineteenth century English artists who sought to represent the religious earnestness of painting before Raphael in works of art which tend to be symbolic and literary.

primary colours in painting terms, red, yellow and blue, from which all other colours can be produced.

quoin-stone stone delineating the external corner in the wall of a building.

ragging paint technique that employs a crumpled piece of rag to create decorative broken-colour finishes.
Raku moulded Japanese earthenware, first produced in the fifteenth century.
rattan palm giving its name to the wickerwork produced from its stems.
Regency English decorative style that absorbed a wide range of contemporary Continental influences. Popular during the early nineteenth century.
Rococo exuberant early eighteenth-century European decorative style characterized by its scalloped curves, elaborate scrolls and pastel colours.
Rustic frivolous eighteenth-century style of decoration applied to both roughly-hewn outdoor furniture and interior plasterwork.

saltglaze slightly pitted glaze applied to stoneware by throwing salt on to the fire of the kiln in which the pots are being baked.
sanguine red chalk containing ferric oxide, used in drawing.
satinwood expensive, hard, pale wood with a satiny grain.
sconce wall-fixed bracket used for holding a candle or light.
scrubbed limewash paint technique that gives walls the appearance of well-scrubbed limewash, which was employed to paint exterior walls.
serpentine marble dark-green or brown patterned stone with veining.
Sèvres porcelain porcelain produced in Sèvres, France, which led European ceramic fashions from 1760 to 1815.
shagreen material created from the dried skins of fish; used in inlays.

Torus moulding on skirting-board

Shaker name of an American sect founded in 1747. The title derives from the excited state of their worship. Their furniture is typified by its functional design and lack of ornament.
shellac varnishing highly skilled sister technique of French polishing.
Siena marble yellow-coloured marble with veining, originating from Siena, a city in Tuscany.

sienna yellowish-brown pigment. The term is a variant of the name of the town, Siena.
sisal robust fibre, used in the manufacture of flooring and rope.
Soane, Sir John (1753–1837) English architect whose approach to interior decor was influenced by Roman and Byzantine architecture.
spattering decorative technique in which a brush, dipped in paint, ink, glaze or varnish, is knocked to spray dots of colour on to a surface.
spectrum colours colours of the rainbow, formed when light is split into its component parts.
spongeware ceramics decorated with colours that are applied with a sponge to give a blotchy effect.
sponging painting technique that uses a damp sponge to produce a mottled, patchy effect.
stencil card stout oiled manila card or thick cartridge paper, from which shapes are cut in order to make stencils.
stencilling method of decoration in which paint is applied through a cut-out design to create images on a surface.
stippling painting or texturing a surface with a fine, mottled pattern, using a stippler or stiff-bristled brush.
stock widest section of the handle of a paintbrush.
stucco fine plaster-type material used both to cover exterior brickwork and to decorate internal walls and ceilings.
sugarsoap alkaline compound used for cleaning or stripping paint.
swag festoon motif, usually representing a line of drapery or a chain of leaves, flowers or fruit.
swatch small piece of material or card used as a sample.

template shape made from paper or card, that acts as a fixed guide for cutting out the same shapes from a variety of other materials.
terracotta literally "cooked earth". High-quality, unglazed fired clay.
terra verde earth colour: Italian for green earth.
ticking stout cotton fabric with a distinctive pattern of narrow stripes.
tie back length of ribbon or cord, or a metal bracket, used to pin a curtain to the side of a window.
tongue-and-groove joint made between two boards by means of a tongue projecting from the edge of one board that slots into a groove along the edge of the other.
torus convex moulding that is semi-circular in cross-section, found on

skirting boards, mouldings, beading and the base of Classical columns.
trefoil arch decorative arch with three arcs arranged in a circle, found in Gothic architecture.
trompe l'oeil any of a variety of optical illusions, such as *grisaille* that are designed, literally, "to trick the eye".

Tongue-and-groove joints in matchboarding

uplighter lamp, often attached to walls, that throws light upwards on to the upper part of walls and the ceiling.

verdigris green colour, produced as a result of naturally-occurring corrosion on copper, bronze and brass.
Victorian Eclectic person who subscribes to the belief that art and interior decoration should draw from a range of different styles.
vignette small illustration that is not contained within a border.
Voysey, Charles Francis (1857–1941) English designer influenced by William Morris, but with a lighter style.

wainscotting lining – usually wood panelling – used to cover the lower wall.
wash thin, home-made paint or diluted, proprietary paint, such as emulsion. Traditionally known as colourwash since it was made by adding colour to limewash.
whitewash see *limewash*.
wickerwork slender, flexible twigs that have been woven together.
window casement window containing frames that are hinged on one side or at the top or bottom.
woodblock block of wood from which a design has been cut. Used for printing an image on to walls or furniture.
woodgraining technique used to imitate the characteristic markings of a variety of natural woodgrains.
Wright, Frank Lloyd (1867–1959) American architect and furniture designer, who cultivated a modern taste for dynamic, angular forms.

ziggurat architectural pyramidal style with castellated edges, popularly adapted into Art Deco.

GUIDE TO SUPPLIERS

General note As well as Crown Berger and F.A. Heffer (listed under Decorating Tools and Materials), suppliers listed on pages 166–69 kindly lent items for photography. Companies that operate a mail order service are indicated ✉

Decorating Tools and Materials

J. W. Bollom
13 Theobald's Road
London WC1X 8FN

SHOWROOM
314–6 Old Brompton Road
London SW5 9JH
General painting supplies, manufacturers of Pervalac crackle medium, range of palette colour emulsions.

C. Brewer
327 Putney Bridge Road
London SW15 2PG
General painting supplies. Branches throughout SE England.

Brodie and Middleton Ltd. ✉
68 Drury Lane
London WC2B 5SP
Decorating brushes, French enamel varnish, glues, metallic powders, paints, pigments and powder colours.

Cornelissen and Son Ltd. ✉
105 Great Russell Street
London WC1B 3RY
Bone glue, brushes, gilding materials, gum arabic, pigments and rabbit-skin glue.

Craig & Rose plc.
172 Leith Walk
Edinburgh EH6 5EB
Extra pale dead-flat varnish, gold leaf, goldsize, specialist brushes and transparent oil glaze. Paint manufacturers; stockists nationwide.

Crown Berger Europe Ltd.
P.O. Box 37
Crown House
Hollins Road
Darwen
Lancashire BB3 0BG
Range of over 600 colours of paint in a choice of finishes for both interior and exterior surfaces.

GENERAL SOURCES

Artists' suppliers The following materials are usually available from good artists' suppliers: artists' acrylics, artists' acrylic varnishes, artists' inks, artists' oil paints, artists' paintbrushes, bone glue, craft knives, goldsize, gouache, gum arabic, metallic paints, modellers' enamel paints, palette knives, poster paints, rabbit-skin glue, scalpels, school powders (non-toxic but not as intense as powder colours), shellac, spray paints, stencil or manila card, universal stainers, wax crayons, writing inks.

DIY stores The following materials, which are used in this book, are usually available from good DIY stores: beeswax furniture polish, button polish, dust mask (paper), dusting brushes, eggshell paint, emulsion paint, EVA, filler, goldsize, hammer-finish enamel paint, knotting, masking tape, mutton cloth, oil-based varnishes, paint buckets, painter's mates, plaster, polyurethane varnish, primers, protective gloves and goggles, PVA, respiratory mask, sand, sanding sealer, sandpaper, scrapers, self-adhesive lead, shellac, smooth-texture coating, solvents, sponges, spray paints, trowels, white polish, wire brushes, wire wool.

Chemists Chemist shops often sell fuller's earth and natural sponges.

Daler-Rowney Ltd. ✉
12 Percy Street
London W1A 2BP
Artists' materials including acetate, acrylic gesso, artists' acrylics, artists' oil paints, gouache, powder colours, stencil card and transfer metal leaf.

Green & Stone ✉
259 King's Road
London SW3 5ER

19 West Market Place ✉
Cirencester
Gloucestershire GLZ 2AE
Artists' materials including acrylic varnish, specialist brushes, casein paints, crackle varnish, gesso and gesso paints, gum arabic, linseed oil, powder colours, shellac, stencilling materials and transparent oil glaze.

W. Habberley Meadows Ltd.
5 Saxon Way
Chelmsley Wood
Birmingham B37 5AY
Artists' brushes, paints and gilding materials.

F. A. Heffer & Sons Ltd.
24 The Pavement
London SW4 0JA
Specialist brushes.

John T. Keep & Sons Ltd. ✉
15 Theobald's Road
London WC1X 8FN
Crackle medium, powder colours, shellac, specialist brushes, transparent oil glaze and universal stainers.

Lyn Le Grice Stencil Design Ltd.
53 Chapel Street
Penzance TR18 4AF
Stencil books, kits and materials. Stencilling courses.

E. Milner Oxford Ltd.
Glanville Road
Cowley
Oxford OX4 2DB
General painting supplies including crackle varnish, specialist brushes, transparent oil glaze and universal stainers.

John Myland ✉
80 Norwood High Street
London SE27 9NW
Artists' brushes, bone glue, French enamel varnish, liming wax, oil-based varnish, palette-colour emulsions (including earth colours), pigments, powder colours, rabbit-skin glue, rottenstone, shellac, transparent oil glaze and universal stainers.

The Paint Service Co. Ltd.
19 Eccleston Street
London SW1 9LX
Specialist brushes, transparent oil glaze and varnishes.

Paper and Paints ⊠
4 Park Walk
London SW10 0AD
Suppliers of many specialist paints and decorating materials and a range of "historic" colours. Colourmatching service available.

E. Ploton (Sundries) Ltd. ⊠
273 Archway Road
London N6 5AA
Artists' materials including acetate, acrylic gesso, acrylic varnish, artists' acrylics, artists' oil paints, crackle varnish, gouache, gum arabic, metallic powders, specialist brushes and transfer metal leaf.

Potmolen Paint
27 Woodcock Industrial Estate
Warminster
Wiltshire BA12 9DX
Specialist paint suppliers including distempers, gilding materials and traditional materials.

J. H. Ratcliffe & Co. (Paints) Ltd. ⊠
135a Linaker Street
Southport PR8 5DF
Brushes and tools for graining, and transparent oil glaze.

Robertson and Co. Ltd.
1a Hercules Street
London N7 6AT
Artists' oil paints, bronze powders, inks, varnishes and watercolours.

Simpsons Paints Ltd.
122–4 Broadley Street
London NW8 8BB
Gold leaf, specialist brushes and transparent oil glaze.

Stuart R. Stevenson
68 Clerkenwell Road
London EC1M 5QA
Artists' and gilding materials.

Lewis Ward & Co.
128 Fortune Green Road
London NW6 1DN
Specialist brushes including Omega, Whistler and foreign brands.

Architectural salvage
The following are an excellent source of reclaimed period fittings, old furniture and unusual "one-offs".

Architectural Antiques
Savoy Showrooms
New Road
South Molton
Devon EX36 4BH
Baths and bathroom furniture, fireplaces and surrounds, pub interiors, panelling and staircases.

Architectural Heritage
Taddington Manor
Taddington
Near Cutsdean
Cheltenham
Gloucestershire GL54 5RY
Fireplaces and surrounds, period panelling produced in a range of woods and stained glass.

Bailey's Architectural Antiques
The Engine Shed
Ashburton Industrial Estate
Ross-on-Wye
Herefordshire HR9 7BW
Carved marble, fireplaces, hand-painted tiles, pews, stained glass and bathrooms.

Cantabrian Antiques and Architectural Furnishings
16 Park Street
Lynton
North Devon EX35 6BY
Baths and bathroom fittings, beams, door furniture, fireplaces, marble surrounds and wood panelling. Unusual items.

Havenplan Ltd.
The Old Station
Station Road
Killamarsh
Sheffield S31 8EN
Architectural furniture, including church furnishings, doors, fireplaces and panelling.

The House Hospital
68 Battersea High Street
London SW11 3HX
Baths and bathroom furniture, brass fittings, cast iron radiators, doors, fireplaces and spindles.

London Architectural Salvage Company
St. Michael and All Angels
Mark Street
London EC2A 4ER
Bathroom and kitchen furniture and fittings, ceramics, doors, shutters, flooring, lighting, metalware, door furniture, panelling and carved woodwork, staircases and spindles.

REFERENCE BOOKS

The Dover Bookshop ⊠
18 Earlham Street, London WC2H 9LN
Reference and stencil books

The Dover Pictorial Archive Series
Decorative Frames and Borders E. V. Gillon Jnr.
Cartouches and Decorative Small Frames E. V. Gillon Jnr.
Pugin's Gothic Ornament A. C. Pugin
Florid Victorian Ornament K. Klimsch
Art Deco Spot Illustrations W. Rowe
Scroll Ornaments of the Early Victorian Period F. Knight
Rustic Vignettes for Artists and Craftsmen W. H. Pyne
Historic Ornament, a Pictorial Archive C. B. Griesbach
Découpage Eleanor Hasbrouck Rawlings

OTHER USEFUL WORKS
History of the English House Nathaniel Lloyd
  Architectural Press Facsimile reprint 1983
Period Houses and their Details Colin Amery
  Architectural Press 1974
A Grammar of Ornament Owen Jones
  Omega Facsimile reprint 1989
Ornament Stuart Durant
  Macdonald 1986
Authentic Decor Peter Thornton
  Weidenfeld and Nicolson 1984

Robertson and Partners
Jodrell Street
Nuneaton
Warwickshire CV11 5EH
Doors, flooring and staircases salvaged from old houses.

Solopark
The Old Railway Station
Station Road
Pampisford
Cambridge CB2 4HB
Architectural antiques, stripped pine doors and flooring tiles.

Andy Thornton Architectural Antiques Ltd.
Ainleys Industrial Estate
Elland
West Yorkshire HX5 9JP
Cast iron baths, doors, fireplaces, pews and revolving doors.

Walcot Reclamation Ltd.
108 Walcot Street
Bath
Avon BA1 5BG
Traditional architectural antiques.

Fabrics and wallpapers

Joanna Booth
247 King's Road
London SW3 5EL
Antique textiles including tapestries, cushions and curtains. Also wood carvings, early oak furniture and old drawings.

Colefax and Fowler
39 Brook Street
London W1Y 2JE
Reproduction 18th and 19th century fabrics and wallpapers, upholstered furniture and decorative accessories.

The Design Archives
79 Walton Street
London SW3 2HP
Curtain material, upholstery fabric and wallpapers produced from original 17th, 18th and 19th century designs.

Gallery of Antique Costume & Textiles
2 Church Street
London NW8 8ED
Antique textiles including costumes, curtains, furnishings, hangings, needlework, quilts, religious vestments and tapestries.

Judy Greenwood Antiques
657 Fulham Road
London SW6 5PY
Antique textiles including paisley and 19th century French curtains and quilts.

Danielle Hartwright
Antique Textiles
Liberty's of Regent Street
Regent Street
London W1R 6AH
Antique Aubusson curtains and pelmets.

Karls ✉
6 Cheval Place
London SW7 1ES
Swedish reproduction fabrics and wallpapers. Supply trade only: write for list of retail outlets.

Laura Ashley
Customer Services
Braywick House
Braywick Road
Maidenhead
Berkshire SL6 1DW
Range of period design and country fabrics and wallpapers. Outlets nationwide.

Ornamenta Ltd.
PO Box No 784
London SW7 2TG
Trompe l'oeil and hand-printed wallpaper decorations, come ready-cut.

Osborne & Little
304–308 King's Road
London SW3 5UH

39 Queen Street
Edinburgh EH2 3NH
Wide range of original, contemporary and Classical fabrics, wallpapers and trimmings. For list of stockists write to Head Office, Osborne & Little, 49 Temperley Road, London SW12 3QE.

Rare Carpets Gallery
45 Fernshaw Road
London SW10 0TN

496 King's Road
London SW10 0LE
Hand-made antique and contemporary carpets, antique furniture and textiles.

Arthur Sanderson & Sons Ltd.
52 Berners Street
London W1P 3AD
Hand-printed wallpapers, co-ordinating ranges of wallpapers, borders, fabrics and voiles. Bed linen, carpets and paints.

Souleiado
171 Fulham Road
London SW3 6JW
Provençal prints on cotton and objects made from cotton fabrics, bed linen and tablecloths.

Stothert & Miles Ltd.
8 Holbein Place
London SW1W 8NL
Reproduction textiles and fabrics of 18th and 19th century country house styles.

Bernard Thorp
6 Burnsall Street
London SW3 3ST
Hand screen-printers and weavers, specializing in custom coloured designs printed on a range of fabrics.

Timney Fowler
388 King's Road
London SW3 5UZ
Contemporary range of black and white furnishing fabrics, wallpapers and borders in a neo-Classical style.

Warner Fabrics plc.
7–11 Noel Street
London W1V 4AL
Traditional and contemporary printed and woven fabrics and wallcoverings.

Watts & Co.
7 Tufton Street
London SW1P 3QE
Reproduction 18th and 19th century fabric designs including gold cloth. Also hand-printed wallpapers, tassels, tiebacks and trimmings. Write for list of stockists.

Flooring

Amtico
17 St. George Street
London W1R 9DE
Manufacturers of quality vinyl tiles for flooring within the home or commercially. See pages 37, 41, 63 and 141 for examples. Write for details of outlets and flooring contractors.

Castlenau Tiles
15 Church Road
London SW13 9HR
Ceramic and terracotta tiles.

Fired Earth
Middle Aston
Oxfordshire OX5 3PX
Hand-made floor and wall tiles.

Paris Ceramics
543 Battersea Park Road
London SW11 3BL
European traditional ceramics including antique terracotta (reclaimed from French country houses) and stone floors.

Furniture and accessories
Antique, reproduction and contemporary merchandise.

David Alexander Antiques
102 Waterford Road
London SW6 2HA
16th–18th century furniture and accessories, and architectural items.

Nick Allen Consultancy
Ground Floor Studio
80b Battersea Rise
London SW11 1EH
Versatile range of steel furniture. Works to commission. Studio collection also available at The Studio, 6 Cale Street, London SW3 3QU.

Philip Allison Antiques & Decorative Arts
The Furniture Cave
533 King's Road
London SW10 0TZ
Antique and reproduction oak and mahogany furniture and accessories.

Maria Andipa Icon Gallery
162 Walton Street
London SW3 2JL
Icons from around the world, country furniture and oil lamps.

Antiquarius
(Banjarah Tent, Chelsea Clocks and Antiques, Persiflage)
131–141 King's Road
London SW3 5ST
Antique furniture, decorative accessories and clocks.

Antique Designs Ltd.
277 Lillie Road
London SW6 7PN
Reproduction furniture in various European styles ranging from Biedermeier to Art Deco.

Antiquus
90–92 Pimlico Road
London SW1W 8PL
Objects, paintings and furniture from the antique world to the 19th century.

K. Armelin Antiques
592 King's Road
London SW6 2DX
English and French 18th and early 19th century furniture.

BDI
The Furniture Cave,
533 King's Road
London SW10 0TZ
Decorative English and continental furniture. Also architectural fitments, sculpture and antique furnishing fabrics.

Mary Bellis Antiques
Charnham Close
Hungerford
Berkshire RG17 0EJ
Quality 16th and 17th century oak furniture and works of art.

Jean Brown
The Furniture Cave
533 King's Road
London SW10 0TZ
Mainly 19th century French decorative furniture, objets d'art and small architectural pieces.

Browns
The Furniture Cave
533 King's Road
London SW10 0TZ
Georgian, Victorian and Edwardian furniture, mirrors, prints and other decorative items.

Carless and Gray
608 King's Road
London SW6 2DZ
Unusual antique and reproduction decorative furniture and accessories.

Decorative Living
55 New King's Road
London SW6 4SE
Antique and Colonial design furniture. Also unusual decorative accessories including lighting.

The Dining Room Shop
62–4 White Hart Lane
London SW13 0PZ
Everything for the dining room, including furniture, china and glass.

Charles Edwards
582 King's Road
London SW6 2DY
Decorative antique furniture, pictures and lighting fixtures.

Five Five Six Antiques
556 King's Road
London SW6 2DZ
Beautiful and unusual objects, furniture and paintings. Antique and contemporary.

Robin Gage
Unit 7
The Talina Centre
23a Bagleys Lane
London SW6 2BW
Reproductions of 18th and 19th century French, Italian and neo-Classical decorative accessories.

The General Trading Company Ltd.
144 Sloane Street
London SW1X 9BL
Household furnishings, china, glass, linen and stationery from all over the world, including antiques and Oriental items.

Graham & Green
4 & 7 Elgin Crescent
London W11 2JA
Antique, reproduction and contemporary decorative and useful accessories. Also furniture, ceramics, glass, textiles and lighting. Brochure available.

Elizabeth Griffiths
Clockwork Studios
38 Southwell Road
London SE5 9PG
Fine artist making papier-mâché vessels.

Hirst Antiques
59 Pembridge Road
London W11 3HN
Four-poster and half-tester antique beds, decorative furniture and objects.

Lacquer Chest
71 & 75 Kensington Church Street
London W8 4BG
Extensive range of esoteric antique objects, including furniture, glasswork, paintings and pottery.

Ligne Roset
132 Shaftesbury Avenue
London W1V 7DN
Extensive range of contemporary upholstery and cabinet systems, with complementary accessories and lighting.

Michael Marriott Ltd.
588 Fulham Road
London SW6 5NT
18th and 19th century furniture and decorative antique prints.

Michael Midgley and Carolyn Cusk Ltd.
13 Hewer Street
London W10 6DU
Hand-painted reproduction 18th and 19th century furniture and accessories.

Richard Miles Antiques
8 Holbein Place
London SW1W 8NL
Antique furniture and decorative accessories from Regency "Gothic" to Colonial Anglo-Indian in exotic woods.

M.S.M. Antiques
The Furniture Cave
533 King's Road
London SW10 0TZ
Antique and reproduction furniture, decorative accessories, fabrics, fireplaces and lighting from all periods.

Neal Street East
5 Neal Street
London WC2H 9PU
Homeware, cookware, lighting, textiles and books from the Orient.

Oggetti
101 Jermyn Street
London SW1Y 6EE
A wide range of contemporary objects and accessories of high-quality design.

Old Pine
594 King's Road
London SW6 2DX
Individually painted antique furniture of French and English origin.

Barrie Quinn Antiques
3–4 Broxholme House
New King's Road
London SW6 4AA
Range of antique furniture, mirrors, decorative accessories and ceramic jardinières.

Rogier Antiques
20a Pimlico Road
London SW1W 8LJ
European antique and reproduction objects, specializing in Provençal style. Also painted, gilded and lacquered work.

Edward Russell Decorative Accessories Ltd.
18–20 Scrutton Street
London EC2A 4RJ
Manufacturers of decorative accessories and lamps.

Santa Fe Trading Post
334 Bruton Place
London W1X 7AA
Traditionally crafted contemporary pine washstands, hand-painted candlesticks.

David Savage Furnituremakers
21 Westcombe
Bideford
North Devon EX39 3JQ
Contemporary hand-crafted furniture made from European hardwoods, polished with natural oils and waxes.

Serena Stapleton Antiques
75 Lower Richmond Road
London SW15 1ET
18th and 19th century decorative furniture, pictures and objets d'art.

Themes and Variations
231 Westbourne Grove
London W11 2SE
Contemporary furniture, decorative accessories and lighting.

Tobias & the Angel
68 White Hart Lane
London SW13 0PZ
Contemporary and antique (country and Victorian) decorative accessories, furniture, garden accessories, kitchenware, lighting and fabrics.

David Weston Ltd.
44 Duke Street
London SW1Y 6DD
Globes, scientific instruments and various marine antiques.

Mark Wilkinson
27 High Street
Bromham
Chippenham
Wiltshire SN15 2HA
Bespoke furniture designers and manufacturers of kitchens, bedrooms and bathrooms. Write for other outlets.

Oscar Woollens Ltd.
81–85 Hampstead Road
London NW1 2PL
Modern furniture from the world's top European and American designers.

Robert Young
68 Battersea Bridge Road
London SW11 3AG
English and European antique country furniture, decorative accessories and stocks of naive and folk art.

Glass and ceramics

Beverly
30 Church Street
London NW8
Antique and contemporary glass and ceramics, specializing in Art Nouveau and Art Deco pieces. Also metalwork.

Isobel Dennis
Clockwork Studios
38 Southwell Road
London SE5 9PG
Bright, contemporary, hand-finished ceramic bowls and dishes with a fruit and floral theme.

Jonathan Horne (Antiques) Ltd.
66c Kensington Church Street
London W8 4BY
Specialists in early English pottery from 17th–19th century including large stocks of 18th century tiles.

Lalique
24 Mount Street
London W1Y 5RB
Importers and distributors of Lalique crystal and Christofle silverware.

The Perfect Glass Shop
5 Park Walk
Fulham Road
London SW10 0AJ
Modern, traditional and antique glassware. Engraving and repairs.

Phillips West Two
10 Salem Road
London W2 4DL
Fine art auctioneers with 44 branches.

Lighting

Fergus Cochrane Antiques
570 King's Road
London SW6 2DY
Antique lighting: wall-lights, sconces, chandeliers, candlesticks and lamp bases.

Jack Casimir Ltd.
23 Pembridge Road
London W11 3HG
16th–19th century antique lighting, fireplace accessories and metalware.

Jones Antique Lighting
194 Westbourne Grove
London W11 2RH
*Antique lighting 1860–1960. Table, wall
and ceiling lights and glass shades.*

Lumineres Ltd.
at Remember Antiques
68 Stanhope Road
St Albans
Hertfordshire AL1 5BL
*Reproduction brass wall lamps and
Griffin table lamps.*

McCloud & Co. Ltd. ⊠
269 Wandsworth Bridge Road
London SW6 2TX
*Decorative metalwork, reproduction and
contemporary designs for furniture and
lighting in patinated steel and other media.*

**Edward Russell Decorative
Accessories**
18–20 Scrutton Street
London EC2A 4RJ
*Hand-made lampshades and wooden
lamp bases. Faux painting, trompe l'oeil
and watercoloured items.*

Tempus Stet Ltd.
Trinity Business Centre
305–309 Rotherhithe Street
London SE16 1EY
*Reproduction lighting and mirrors in a
range of finishes. Write for local stockists.*

**Christopher Wray's Lighting
Emporium**
600 King's Road
London SW6 2DX
*Antique and reproduction lighting. Write
for details of other outlets.*

Metalwork

Freud
198 Shaftesbury Avenue
London WC2H 8JL
*Contemporary steel candlesticks and a
range of metal furniture.*

Ikon Corporation
B5L Metropolitan Wharf
Wapping Wall
London E1 9SS
Contemporary accessories in aluminium.

The Light Shop
34–48 Turnham Green Terrace
London W4 4PL
Contemporary metal candlesticks.

Peter Place Antiques
636 King's Road
London SW6 2DU
*Antique and reproduction iron chandeliers
and wall sconces. Also 19th century
ceramics and decorative country artefacts.*

Mouldings and timber

Daler-Rowney Ltd. ⊠
12 Percy Street
London W1A 2BP
*Manufacturers of lincrusta friezes and
dados.*

E. J. Harmer & Co. Ltd.
19a Birbeck Hill
London SE21 8JS
*Able to reproduce all periods of
plasterwork.*

George Jackson & Sons
Unit 19
Mitcham Industrial Estate
Streatham Road
Mitcham
Surrey CR4 2AJ
*Plasterwork and composition details from
18th century mouldings.*

Locker & Riley Ltd.
Capital House
Bruce Grove
Wickford
Essex SS11 8DB
*Manufacturers and installers of fibrous
plasterwork designs of all periods.*

The Newson Group
190 Ebury Street
London SW1 8UP
*Wide range of materials for decoration
including timber, mouldings, doors and
windows, fireplaces and accessories,
flooring, plasterwork, plumbing and
decorating tools, materials and
accessories. Catalogue available.
Examples of materials used: pierced
screen on page 54; cornice, panelling
and banister on page 64; dado rail on
page 84.*

Oakleaf Reproductions Ltd. ⊠
Ling Bob Mills
Main Street
Wilsden
Bradford
Yorkshire BD15 0JP
Quality hand-stained mouldings in rigid

*polyurethane foam of highly ornate and
detailed woodwork. For examples
see panelling on page 68, frieze on
page 110.*

Thames Moulding Company
16b Whytecliffe Road
Purley
Surrey CR2 2AU
Historically accurate period mouldings.

Paintings and prints

ARC Prints and Frames
26 North Street
London SW4 0HB
*Decorative 17th–19th century
reproduction prints, specializing in
architecture. Expert framing service.*

Norman Blackburn
32 Ledbury Road
London W11 2AB
*Interesting old prints (1600–1860) in
period frames.*

Corporate Fine Art
24 Cale Street
Chelsea Green
London SW3 3QU
*Fine antique prints and maps,
specializing in London items.*

Crane Gallery
171a Sloane Street
London SW1X 9QG
*High-quality American and British
folk art.*

Stern Art Dealers
46 Ledbury Road
London W11 2AB
*Large stock of 19th and early 20th century
English and European oil paintings.*

Plumbing fitments

C. P. Hart & Sons Ltd.
Newnham Terrace
Hercules Road
London SE1 7DR
*High-quality bath and kitchen products in
traditional and contemporary styles.*

Sitting Pretty Ltd.
131 Dawes Road
London SW6 7EA
*Traditional and classical bathrooms,
accessories including bathracks, towels and
hand-painted mirrors.*

INDEX

A

acetate, stencils, 38, 130
acetone, 142, 154
Adam, Robert, 16, 42, 160
ageing and antiquing,
        62–73, 160
        craquelure effect,
        66–67
        gold, 102
        metals, 41
        paint on wood, 36
                techniques, 68–69
        plaster walls, 30
                techniques, 70–71
        plasterwork, 33
                techniques, 55,
                68–69
        using glazes and
                waxes, 54,
                68–69, 144, 159
        wallpapers, 60
American styles:
        New England
        living room, 98
        Santa Fe dining
        room, 52
        Shaker style, *22*
aniline dye, 155, 160
anthemion, 41, 43, 160
antiquing *see* ageing and
        antiquing
arabesque, 160
architraves, 160
armillary spheres, 160
armoires, 160
Art Deco, 160
artists' acrylic paints, 138,
        148, 154–55, 157
artists' oil paints, 136,
        148–51, 152–53,
        157
Art Nouveau, 160
        frieze, 102–103

Arts and Crafts movement,
        14, 15, 160
ash wood, 35
Australian balcony, 72
Aztecs, 160

B

"bagging", 56
bain-marie, 156–58, 160
Bakelite, 160
balcony, Australian, 72
Baroque,
        drawing room, 50
        bedroom, 86, 118
bas-relief, 160
bathrooms:
        Biedermeier, 70, 94
        Greco-Roman, 48
Bauhaus, 160
beading, 160
bedheads,
        craquelure finish, 66
beeswax furniture polish:
        antiquing wax,
        68–69, 144, 159
        buying and storing,
        158
        composition and
        properties, 154–55
        finish for wood, 34
Biedermeier style, 94, 160
        bathroom, 70, 94
binders in paints, 136, 138
borders:
        paper, 38
        stencilling, 112
Boucher, François, 160
Brescia marble, 160
        techniques, 90
bridges, stencils, 110, 115
brocade, 160

brown paper, 39
brushes, 122–29
        artists', 125
        care of, 134–35
        dusting, 126–27
        emulsion, 123
        fitch, 124–25
        lily-bristle, 122–23,
        126–27
        lining, 124
        sable, 124
        sash, 123
        for softening,
        126–27
        spattering, 60–61
        for specialist
        techniques,
        128–29
        for stencilling, 128
        for stippling, 128
        swordlinder, 124
        for varnishing, 126
        woodgraining
        with, 96–97
burr wood finish,
        clair bois, 95
butter muslin, 160
Byzantine art, 160

C

cabriole legs, 160
cachepot, 160
calico, 160
card, 38–39
Caribbean style, 21
Carrara marble, 160
        techniques, 88–89
cartouches, 118, 160
caryatids, 160
castellation, 160
casting plaster, 33
ceilings, colour, 18
        see also cornices

censer, 160
ceramic suppliers, 168
Cézanne, Paul, 160
CFC (chloroflurocarbon),
        138,160
cheesecloth, 160
chevrons, 160
Chinoiserie, 160
chintz, 160
chisel head brushes,
        122–123, 160
clair bois, 160, 94–95
cleaning brushes, 134–35
Cliff, Clarice, 160
Colours:
        complementary,
        24, 160
        earth colours, 137
        historical, 16–17
        lighting and, 24–25
        pigments, 148–51
        primary, 162
        swatches, 14–15, 163
        transparent oil
        glaze, 54, 157
        whole house
        treatment, 26
colourwashing, 160
        recipes, 157
                techniques, 46–51
        three-colour, 45
                techniques, 48–49
        wood, 36, 44
                techniques, 50–51
combination gilding, 146,
        160
combing, 129, 160
techniques, 56, 57
complementary colours,
        24, 160
composition, 161
Cooper, Susie, 161
copper, 40
corbels, 33, 161

cornices, 161
for dividing wall
space, 18
structural
features, 20–21
cracked lacquer:
paint effect, 63
recipe, 156
craquelure, 62, 161
crackle varnish, 140
techniques, 66–67
recipe, 156
see also cracked
lacquer
creamware, 161

d

dado, 160
dividing wall
space, 18–19
rails, 18–19,
20–21, 161
damask, 161
découpage, 38–39, 161
techniques,
116–117
see also photocopies
Delfware, 161
Della Robbia ceramics,
161
dentil, 161
dentilled cornice,
20–21
distemper, 161
colourwashing
with, 46
composition and
properties, 152–53
recipe, 156
dragging, 56, 161
dry-brushing, 161
techniques, 52–53
dusting brushes, 127
dust mask, 29
using with gesso, 100

dust masks cont.
using with metallic
powder, 102–103
using with
powder colours, 149

e

earth colours, 137, 161
ebony, imitating, 161
egg-and-dart pattern, 161
eggshell paint, 139
composition and
properties, 152–53
tinting, 157
Empire style, 161
colours, 16
emulsion paint, 139
brushes for, 123
colourwashing
with, 46
composition and
properties, 152–53
recipe for washes, 157
stencilling, 112
tinting, 157
enamel paint, hammer-
finish, 41, 139
enamel varnish *see* French
enamel varnish
English Baroque parlour, 50
engravings, 116–17
environmental issues, 159
equipment *see* tools

f

fabric suppliers, 166
faience, 161
faux effects, 74–107, 161
Brescia marble,
90, 160
Carrara marble,
88–89, 160
clair bois, 94–95
fossilstone marble,

faux effects cont.
92–93
iron, 40, 86–87
lead, 82
leather, 75, 80–81
materials, 144
pietra serena, 76–77
plaster, 82
sandstone, 78–79, 145
serpentine marble,
88–89, 163
Siena marble, 75,
90–91
stained glass, 42,
106–107
terracotta, 75, 82–83
see also gilding; rust
effects; verdigris;
woodgraining
ferrules, 161
filigree, 161
finials, 161
finish, for varnished
paintwork, 159
fitches, 124–25
flagged bristles, 122, 161
fleur-de-lys, 161
stencils, 130–31
flogging brushes, 129
floors:
suppliers, 166–67
wood-effect, 36
fly-spots, imitating, 62, 66,
161
fossilstone marble, 161
techniques, 92–93
French colours, 16
French Empire scheme, 56
French enamel varnish, 141
antiquing with, 41
composition and
properties, 154–55
patinating gold
with, 104–105
recipe, 156
French kitchen, 112
French polishing, 141, 161
frescoes, 32, 161

friezes, 161
lincrusta, 42
wrapping paper, 12
furniture:
Biedermeier style, 94
Lloyd Loom, 162
suppliers, 167–68

g

gesso, 144
composition and
properties,
152–53
gilding over,
100–101, 146
recipe, 156
gilding, 40–41, 161
with Dutch metal,
100–101, 146
gold leaf, 100, 146
materials, 146–47, 158
metallic powders,
102–103, 158
patinated gold,
104–105
plaster, 32
techniques, 100–103
tools, 128
transfer leaf, 100,
146–47
Gill, Eric, 161
gingham, 161
glass, 42
stained, 42, 106–107
suppliers, 168
glazework:
antique finishes,
67–68
materials, 140–41
patterned, 56–57
protecting, 158
softened, 54–55
glue-based paints, 137
glues:
bone glue,
136–37, 158

buying and
storing, 158
gelatin-based,
137, 158
rabbit-skin, 100,
137, 144, 146
buying and
storing, 158
recipe, 156
see also PVA
gold·*see* gilding
goggles, 29, 92, 102–103,
104
goldsize, 140, 146–147,
154–55
gilding
techniques, 100,
102–103
Gothic arch, 161
Gothick style, 161
bathroom, 116
Gothic Revival, 161
gouache, 138, 152–53, 161
graining *see* woodgraining
granite effect, spattering,
60
Greco-Roman bathroom,
48
grisaille, 161
techniques,
118–19
Gropius, Walter, 161
gum arabic,
recipe, 156
gypsum plaster, 144, 161

h

half tone, 161
hammer-finish enamel
paint, 41, 139
hardwoods, 34, 35
hemp scrim, 30, 161
hessian, 161
horizontal rhythms, 22–23

i

icons, 161
inks, 138
inlays, 161
inspiration, sources of,
14–15
iron:
paint effects, 41
techniques, 86–87

j

jamb dusters, 127

k

Kandinsky, Wassily, 162
kelims, 162
Klee, Paul, 162
Knotting, 34, 36, 154–55

l

lacquerwork, 162
cracked paint
effect, 63, 156
Lalique, René, 162
Landseer, Sir Edwin
Henry, 162
Langley, Batty, 162
lapis lazuli, 162
lead:
self-adhesive,
106–107
techniques, 82
leather:
paint effect, 75
techniques, 80–81
lighting:
colour and mood,
24–25

lighting cont.
suppliers, 168–69
lily-bristle brushes,
122–24, 126–27
limestone effect, 76
limewash, 162
composition and
properties, 152–53
see also scrubbed
limewash
liming paste, 157
liming wax, 58–59, 159
recipe, 156–57
liming wood, 36–37, 162
materials, 145
techniques, 58–59
lincrusta, 42, 162
painting, 108
linenfold panelling, 162
lining brushes, 124
lining paper, 38–39, 159
Living rooms:
New England
living room, 98
Scottish sitting
room, 78, 96
Shaker parlour, 22
Tudor reception, 80
Lloyd Loom furniture, 162
low relief *see* bas relief

m

Mackintosh, Charles
Rennie, 106–107, 162
majolica, 162
manila card, stencils, 38,
110–11, 115, 130–31,
156
marbling, 31, 162
Brescia, 160
techniques, 90
Carrara, 160
techniques, 88–89
fossilstone, 161
techniques, 92–93
serpentine, 163
techniques, 88–89

marble cont.
Siena, 163
techniques, 90–91
marquetry, 162
masking tape, 132
masks (card), 130, 162
techniques, 80–81
masks (protective):
dust, 29, 100,
102–103, 149
respiratory, 29,
104, 152
matchboarding, 21, 162
materials:
buying and storing,
158
gilding, 146–47
paints, 136–39
pastes and powders,
144–45
solvents, 142–43
suppliers, 164–65
varnishes and glazes,
140–41
Mayan, 162
memento mori, 162
metallic paints, 41
metallic powders:
buying and
storing, 158
gilding with, 147,
102–103
quantities, 159
metalwork:
antiquing, 41
faux effects, 84–87
finishes, 40–41
priming, 40
protecting, 40
suppliers, 169
methylated spirits, 142,
143, 154
milk paint, 162
mirrors, 42
mitre joints, 162
Modernism, 162
mood, lighting and, 24–25
Moorish, style, 162

Morris, William, 12, 162
mosaic, 162
mouldings:
    authentic, 20–21
    imitating, with
    paint, 118–20
    plaster, 31, 32, 33
    plastic, 33
    suppliers, 169
    wooden, 34
murals, 109
muslin, 162
mutton cloth, 133, 162

n

neo-Classic style, 162
    colours, 16
        mouldings, 21
New Bauhaus, 162
New England living
    room, 98

O

oak, 35
oak-grain effect, 95
obelisks, 80–81, 162
Odeon wall lamps, 162
ogee, 34, 162
ogive arches, 162
oil-based paints, 136, 139,
    152–53
oil-based varnishes, 140
oil glaze *see* transparent
    oil glaze
onyx, 162
ormolu, 162

P

paint effects:
    ageing wood, 37
        techniques, 64–65
    antiquing, 68–69
    "bagging", 56
    Brescia marble,

paint effects cont.
    techniques, 90
    Carrara marble,
        techniques, 88–89
    clair bois,
        techniques, 94–95
    combing, 56, 57
    dragging,
        techniques, 56
    fossilstone marble,
        techniques, 92–93
    granite effect,
        techniques, 60
    grisaille, 118–19, 161
    iron effect, 40
        techniques, 86–87
    lead effect,
        techniques, 82
    leather effect,
        techniques, 80–81
    pietra serena,
        techniques, 76–77
    porphyry,
        techniques, 60
    ragging, 56, 57
    rust, 40
        techniques, 86–87
    sandstone,
        techniques, 78–79
    scrubbed
    limewash,
        techniques, 52–53
    serpentine
    marble, 88–89
    Siena marble,
        techniques,
        90–91
    softened glazework,
        techniques, 54–55
    spattering,
        techniques, 60–61
    sponging,
        techniques, 46, 56
    terracotta,
        techniques, 82–83
    trompe l'oeil, 120
    see also colourwashing;
    verdigris;

paint effects cont.
    woodgraining
painted pattern, 108–109
paints:
    composition and
    properties, 152–53
    home-made, 136–37
    metallic, 41
    pigments, 148–51
    proprietary, 138–39
    protecting
    finishes, 158
    quantities, 159
    recipes for, 156–57
    for stencilling,
    112, 114
    storing and
    disposing, 158–59
    tinting, 157
panel moulding, 120, 162
panelling,
    rhythms, 22
paper, 38–39
    brown, 39
    découpage, 38–39
        techniques,
        116–17
    glazed, 54–55
    lining, 38–39, 159
    oiled, 38, 156
    printed, 54–55
    see also photocopies
papier-mâché, 42, 162
parlours:
    English Baroque, 50
    Shaker, 20
parquetry, 162
pastes, 144–45
patinas, 41, 162
    antiquing, 55
    gold, 104–105
pattern books, 165
pattern glazework,
    techniques, 56–57
pelmets, 162
period houses, 26
photocopies, 108
    for borders, 38

photocopies cont.
    colour, 39
    découpage, 38–39
    and stencilling, 131
    techniques, 116–17
pickled wood, 36, 162
    technique, 58
picture frames,
    grisaille, 118
picture rails, 162
picture suppliers, 169
pietra serena, 162
    techniques, 76–77
pigments, 17, 136–37
    characteristics,
    148–51
    home-made paints,
    136–37
pilasters, 162
Piranesi, Giovanni
    Battista, 120, 162
plaster:
    ageing walls, 30
        techniques, 72–73
    antiquing, 33
        techniques, 70–71
    casting, 33
    composition, 21,
    42, 161
    decorating, 32–33
    drying out, 32
    filling, 30
    flat, 30
    frescoes, 32
    gilding, 32
    materials, 144
    mixing, 30
    mouldings, 20, 31,
    32, 33
    paint effect, 33, 82
    preparation, 30, 32
    protecting
    finishes, 158
    quantities, 159
    stabilizing, 30
    storing, 158
    tinting and powder
    colours, 32, 157

plaster cont.
types, 32
plastic, 42–43
    mouldings, 33
plumbing, suppliers, 169
porphyry, 162
    techniques, 60
porticoes, 162
poster paints, 139
powder colours:
    buying and
    storing, 158
    composition and
    properties, 152–53
    for home-made
    paints, 136
    recipes using, 156–57
    safety, 149
powders:
    gilding, 147
    metallic, 102–103,
    147, 158
Pre-Raphaelite
    brotherhood, 162
primary colours, 162
primers, 40, 138
prints, suppliers, 169
protecting paint
    finishes, 158
PVA:
    colourwashing, 46
    composition and
    properties, 152–53
    gesso, 100–101,
    144, 146
    in home-made
        paints, 137
    preparing plaster
    with, 32
    varnishes, 141
    water-based wash,
    46–47, 48–49,
    92–93, 157

q
quantities, calculating, 159

quoin-stones, 163

r
ragging, 56, 57, 163
rails:
    dado, 18–19,
    20–21, 161
    picture, 162
Raku, 163
rattan furniture, 163
recipes, 156–57
reference sources, 14
Regency style, 163
    colours, 16
repainting surfaces, 159
resin, cast, 36, 42
respiratory mask, 104
rhythm, *22–23*
rockers, 129
    woodgraining
    with, 98–99
Rococo style, 163
    colours, 17
rollers:
    special, 128
        techniques, 95
    standard, 28
ropes, 32, 43
rubber stamps, 131
rust:
    decorative effects, 40
    materials, 145
    paint effect, 40–41
        techniques, 74,
        86–87
    preventing, 40
Rustic styles, 163

s
safety:
    paints, 150–51, 152
    powder colours,
    149, 150–51
    solvents, 142, 152
    varnishes, 152–53
saltglaze, 163

sand texture, 145
sanding sealer, 58, 102,
    141, 154–55
sandpaper, 133
sandstone:
    materials, 145
    techniques, 78–79
sanguine, 163
Santa Fe dining room, 52
satinwood, 94, 163
scagliola, 31
sconces, 163
Scottish sitting room, 78,
    96
scrapers, 132
scrubbed limewash:
    paint effect, 45, 163
    techniques, 52–53
serpentine marble:
    paint effect, 163
    techniques, 88–89
Sèvre porcelain, 163
shagreen, 163
Shakers, 163
    mouldings, 20
    parlour, *22*
shellac, 141
    antiquing
plasterwork, 70–71
    brushes, 126
    buying and storing,
    158
    composition and
    properties, 154–55
    sealing plaster, 32
    varnishing, 141, 163
Siena marble, 75, 163
    techniques, 90–91
silicone carbide paper, 101
sisal, 163
slate tiles, 31
Soane, Sir John, 163
softened glazework,
    techniques, 54–55
softening brushes, 126–27
softwoods, 34
solvents:
    cleaning brushes

solvents cont.
    with, 134–35
    disposal of, 159
    paint effects with,
    142–43
    paints and, 138, 153
    safety, 142, 152
    types, 142–43, 154
Spanish Baroque bedroom,
    86, 118
spattering,
    paint effect, 163
    safety, 142
    techniques, 60–61
sponges, 133
spongeware, 163
sponging:
    paint effect, 56, 163
    techniques, 46
spray paints, 138, 152–53
stained glass, 42
    techniques, 106–107
stainers, universal, 136,
    139, 154–55, 157
"stamped" leather, 80–81
stamps, rubber, 131
stencilling, 109, 163
    brushes for, 128, 131
    colourwashing, 49
    effects, 114–15
    friezes, 115
    making stencils
    for, 110–11
    materials, 38
    stencil card, 38,
    110–11, 115,
    130–31, 156, 163
    storing stencils, 158
    techniques, 112–13
    tools, 128, 130–31
stippling:
    brushes for, 128
    paint effect, 163
    wiping and, 55
stock, paint brushes, 127,
    163
stone, 31
stone effects, 74

stone effects cont.
    pietra serena, 76–77
    sandstone, 78–79
storing materials, 158
structural features, 20–21
stucco, 163
stuccowork, imitation, 32
sugarsoap, 36, 163
suppliers, 164–69
swags, 163
swatches, colour, 14–15, 163
swordliners, 124

t

templates, 163
terraccota, 163
    paint effect, 75
        techniques, 82–83
    tiles, 31
terra verde, 163
textiles *see* fabrics
three-colour colourwashing *see* colourwashing
ticking, 163
tiebacks, 163
tiles:
    plastic, 43
    slate, 31
    terracotta, 31
tinting media, recipes, 157
tissue paper, oiled, 39
tongue-and-groove, 21, 163
tools:
    brushes, 122–129, 134–35
    scrapers, 132
    stencils, 130–31
    suppliers, 164–65
torus, 163
tracing paper, 38, 108
transfer leaf, 100, 146–47
transparent oil glaze, 140
    buying and storing, 158

transparent oil glaze cont.
    composition and properties, 154–55
    decorating over, 159
    on lining paper, 159
    for marbling, 88–91
    for patterned glazework, 56–57
    with pigments, 136
    preparation for, 159
    protecting, 158
    recipe, 156
    removing, 159
    softened glazework, techniques, 54–55
    tinting, 157
trefoil arches, 163
trompe l'oeil, 163
    grisaille, 118–19
    techniques, 118–21
    using photocopies, 116
Tudor style, mouldings, 20
turpentine, 142, 154

u

universal stainers, 136, 139, 154–55, 157
uplighters,163

v

varnishes, 140–41
    brushes for, 126
    on colourwashed wood, 50
    composition and properties, 154–55
    crackle, 66–67, 140
    keying, 159
    for protecting paint finishes, 158
    removing, 36, 159
    for softened glazework, 54

varnishes cont.
    storing, 158
    tinting, 157
    for wood, 34
    see also French enamel varnish
verdigris, 40–41, 163
    paste, 145
    techniques, 84–85
Victorian Eclectic, 163
vignettes, 163
Voysey, Charles, 163

w

wainscotting, 163
wallpapers, 38–39
    antiquing, 60
    colours, 17
    suppliers, 166
washes, 163
    emulsion, 46–47, 48–49,50–51
        recipe for, 157
    PVA water-based, 46–47, 48–49, 92–93
        recipe for, 157
    protecting, 158
    water-based (powder colour), 46, 48–49, 50–51, 94–95
        recipe for, 157
    see also colourwashing
water, as solvent, 143
water-based varnishes, 141
waxes, 144
    ageing plaster walls, 70–71
    antiquing techniques, 68–69, 159
    liming, 58–59, 145, 156–57
    quantities, calculating, 159
waxes cont.

    removing, 159
    storing, 158
white spirit, 142, 154
whitewash *see* limewash
whole house treatments, 26–27
wicker furniture, 163
windows, casements, 163
wood:
    ageing paint on, 36
        techniques, 64–65
    clair bois effect, techniques, 94–95
    colourwashing, 36, 44
        techniques, 50–51
    decorating, 36–37
    imitation, 36
    liming, 37
        techniques, 58–59
    mouldings, 20, 34
    natural, 34–35
    preparation, 34–35, 36–37
    suppliers, 169
    types of, 34–35
    varnishing, 34
woodgraining:
    brushes for, 129
    paint effect, 74, 163
    techniques, 37, 94–99
woodstain, 156
Wright, Frank Lloyd, 163

z

ziggurats, 163

ACKNOWLEDGMENTS

Stylist (furnishings and accessories)
Lucinda Egerton

Decorative painters
led by *Erin Sorensen:*
Jane Higginbottom
Julia Last
Sophie Lightfoot
Sarah Mander

Author's acknowledgments
I would like to thank Michael Crockett for his patience and understanding and the editorial team at Dorling Kindersley who have given their all to this project for one and a half years: Rosie, Steve, Mark and Sarah. Also, thanks to Simon Kenny for his supervision of site work while I was working on this book, and especially to my Editor, David Lamb, for developing the idea for this book and for smoothing the path at every stage. Finally, I owe a debt of gratitude to my wife for her patience, help and understanding.

Dorling Kindersley would like to thank the following people: Katherine Townshend for her help with the photography; Crown Paints for supplying paint; The Newson Group for timber and other materials; Brian's Props & Locations for transport; and Sarah Whelan, and The Stylists for additional styling. Also, Hilary Bird for the index; Liza Bruml, Josephine Buchanan, Ruth Carim, Heather Dewhurst, Lesley Ellis, Claire Mitchison and Roger Smoothy for their help with the text; and Michel Blake and Teresa Solomon for production.